CROSSING ROUGH WATERS

Journey from Fear to Freedom

ADVANCE PRAISE

"We appreciate the generosity of Sarah's sharing of practical wisdom in *Crossing Rough Waters –Journey from Fear to Freedom;* it is what we need to remind ourselves of and reawaken to each day. Her insights are refined in the common fire of suffering, from which springs the Phoenix bird of new life. Now the help that she gives to those she counsels is available to thousands of persons who can find their way past clouds of confusion into the clear sky of Spirit."

Harvey and Julie Grady, Center for Human Potential

In *Crossing Rough Waters – Journey from Fear to Freedom,* Sarah Payne Naylor reflects on the vulnerabilities that diminish the way we see ourselves; and reminds us again and again of our fundamental value and worth. In the affirmations that are at the center of this work, she invites us to see ourselves as women and men who are woven through with gifts and strengths that have the power to change our lives and the world around us. Ms. Naylor's commitment is to empower each one of us to consider the possibility of something new.

Dr. Adele Stiles Resmer

If you have never felt special, gifted, unique and valued, this book may be your answer. *Crossing Rough Waters – Journey from Fear to Freedom* presents a reality that often is denied and unwelcome in our childhood. Each one of us is special and a gift to the world. Once I awakened to the profound truth,

i

the messages in this book, that I am a gift and must value my purpose on this earth, my life became illuminated with more light and love than ever before. It doesn't matter who you are, what you have or what you've done, you are a gift. You have something to give that only you can give. I understand now that it is time for me to live as the gift that I am and embrace all the unique, special people in my life, daily. We are all God's Gift in the World.

Sandy Stokes, Retired Bank Vice President

Crossing Rough Waters – Journey from Fear to Freedom is a message of empowerment which, if taken in, can help our spirit breathe and become our full majesty. Reading it reminded me of the many graces I have been given to use in this present journey.

Janet K. Regner, Consultant

Crossing Rough Waters – Journey from Fear to Freedom helps me focus on those things most important about my life from a spiritual and philosophical perspective. I think about what is most important every day.

Delstene Atkinson, Foundation Development Director

CROSSING ROUGH WATERS

Journey from Fear to Freedom

Sarah Payne Naylor

Moonhawk Communications
a program of The Naylor Group, LLC

To Ed

TABLE OF CONTENTS

x

FOREWORD
David Borchard, Ed.D.

Author of *The Joy of Retirement* and *Will the Real You Please Stand Up?*

Crossing Rough Waters – Journey from Fear to Freedom is more than another self-help book. It is a wisdom guide. The source of wisdom is Sarah, a life coach whose advanced professional training comes from the graduate school of life. In this book, Sarah shares stories of her journey with a wit and wisdom that will make you laugh and cry, but more than that, it will teach you invaluable lessons about creating and sustaining a successful life. This is not a book to read and set aside; it is one you'll want to revisit often as a resource to enjoy and to apply the storehouse of insights that Sarah makes available from the trials, tribulations and joys of her own life and her extensive life coaching experience. When life presents you with severe challenges, you either sink from them or grow. Sarah not only grew from her challenges, she transcended them. In this book, she shows you how you too can enhance your life's journey through the lessons she has discovered from her own life and her years of coaching experience. If you are seeking more joy in your life and possess the courage to realize your potential and to grow, this is a book you will treasure.

David Borchard, Ed.D.
Career/Executive Coach and Author

INTRODUCTION

Crossing Rough Waters – Journey from Fear to Freedom is an account of one person's journey through the rough waters of life. Living from a fear-based perspective was woven into the fabric of my life from such an early age that the core of my solar plexus was always in knots and my stomach was often in incredible pain. But, I did not know how to release this pain and fear nor did I understand that these knots were caused by attitudes and behaviors of people who loved me and whom I loved.

The intention to change my life came when I was in my mid-thirties after reading *You Can Heal Your Life* by Louise Hay. She said that in order to heal yourself you must be willing to change, not knowing where that change will lead you. From the moment I read those words I made the decision to go on the journey of healing myself. I did not want to feel that physical pain anymore. I had no idea that I would have to face so many issues in my life that required healing. Little did I know that I would have to confront difficult truths about family relationships and that I would have to face my own behaviors that were not in my own best interest; e.g. lack of confidence, self-esteem, inability to set boundaries, etc.

During this period of personal assessment and change, I learned that I was constantly being prepared to coach others about their issues because I had gone through similar life and career issues that my clients experienced. I understood that there would be an enormous amount of self love and compassion required of oneself in order to cross the rough waters. I knew that it would be no easy feat, even though I felt it would be well worth the effort.

On my life journey I have been introduced to a number of different beliefs; some I have incorporated into my spiritual practice. I have been open to learning about various belief systems from around the world, and I have been fortunate to visit many places that I never would have imagined possible had I not begun my journey of self healing. I have been exposed to different religious and spiritual practices that other cultures live every day but which were different than those I had experienced in the United States. These journeys to foreign lands have opened me to consider the diversity of people, vegetation, and animal life, the geography and geology of the planet, and so much more than I can possibly comprehend. The earth is vast and yet it is a small speck inside of a much larger solar system, and perhaps beyond. I am humbled when I contemplate it. I have come to have such respect for all life and the miracle that it is.

When I lived in the East, I was introduced to a Native American concept and prayer that encompasses this wholeness of thought in which humans are related to everything and everyone. As you begin to read *Crossing Rough Waters — Journey from Fear to Freedom*, consider the scope and power of this life that we are living. Consider that our lives are much bigger than where we stand at this very moment and that our thoughts and prayers have the ability to influence more than we know. We are sacred beings with the ability to love fully, and from that place of love we have the power to change things. Investing in ourselves to heal the pain and fear that has kept us from living our best life is necessary for us as individuals. More than that, ridding ourselves of pain and fear so that we can embrace love in our heart is necessary for the planet. This work we do for ourselves leads us to a life of personal freedom.

Living with love in our heart is a constant goal that is important to strive for. To assist me on this journey the concept of *All My Relations* has been an integral part in my healing and growth. I share this concept with you through an article written by Andrea Lord for *News from Indian Country.*

All My Relations

In the sweat lodges where I reconnected to my culture, it's uttered by the leader as he splatters water on red-hot stone, All My Relations. When the sacred pipe is passed around a circle and the steam is raised to all directions in benediction, the words are there. When the people gather in a good way, each speaker begins with the salutatory statement: ALL MY RELATIONS.

For Natives across Canada, it's the language of communion. It's the recognition of unity in the universe, of harmony, balance and the invisible bridges that span the diversity of our lives; it's a dedication, a greeting, a salutation and a prayer.

…Everything in the universe is in relationship with everything else. Just as the four-leggeds depended upon the waters so, too, did the winged ones, the two-leggeds, the fishes and the plant beings. Life itself was a circle and, for a circle to be complete, it must include everything. And so it was seen that all things are related.

All my relations. I believe that a life based on this premise is salvation for all of us, that political problems are nothing when nations remember their relatedness, that there are no colors or differences, merely one universal heartbeat echoing for all of us.

Eagle Feathers: to all my relations of every nation for their contribution to this life.

HOW THIS BOOK CAME TO BE

How This Book Came to Be

I have only met Jo one time, and this was her message to me: *"When you have crossed the rough waters of life and have made it to the other side of the river with your back still straight, you have a responsibility to tell others about the journey. Where is the book that you have been told to write?"* Jo told me that if I didn't write this book, she would send her posse after me.

In the process of writing this book, there were two symbols that held great significance for me: I had struggled to cross the rough rivers of life to reach the other side with a back that is still straight, and, the butterfly which represented new life because symbolically I felt like I had transitioned from being in a cocoon to becoming a butterfly.

My husband, Ed, and I met Jo and her husband while we were on a recent cruise. The trip was to be a study tour of the life of St. Paul. The journey took us to Turkey and Greece. At the time of this statement from Jo, we were sitting in the ship's captain's quarters where just a few guests had been invited to have cocktails before dinner. Ed and I were quite surprised and honored by this invitation. Prior to the captain joining us at his table, Jo began asking me about who I am. She did not let me finish my personal introduction before she was asking me about the book that I was supposed to write. She was evidently in tune with me, more than I realized.

I had been told several times by other people that I was *supposed* to write a book. It was happening again, in a place where I was not known by anyone. I was shocked.

Even though I had received this message from other people, from my fearful perspective I thought I didn't have anything to say. I thought, who would care, and who would read a book that I wrote. I have finally come to trust and pay attention to my own intuitive messages. The most recent time that I received a message about writing a book was in a dream. After Jo's admonition, I decided to pay attention.

The dream message I received was this, *"Be reminded. You are God's gift to the world. You have been created for this special work as you walk upon the earth. You are to be who you are, your unique self. It is the reason you are here at this moment. Whatever your life situation is, you must gather the courage to move past your fears. Be the person you want to see in the world. Live in love and the light of God. Stop trying to be accepted by everyone. Be the unique person that you are and then be in service with that gift, because your time is NOW!"*

The dream told me that all of us are to be reminded daily that we are each God's gift to the world, no matter what. *"This dream comes through you for a purpose. You are to give the message to others. This message is for everyone in the world."* This was the last thing I heard.

When I awakened from the dream, I was trembling. I hurriedly wrote the words down on paper. I knew that the message was as true for me as it was for everyone. I had been told in the dream that this message was the subject for my book. In that instant, I realized that my whole life had been in preparation for this moment; the good, the bad, and the ugly. I was

4

to live my life released from the fear that I had been carrying all of my life. I was supposed to trust that all would be well.

Most of my life I had lived in fear, in the insecurity that I wasn't enough and didn't measure up. I was told that I did not have the "right" credentials; I wasn't the "right" color and ethnic group (I am an African-American woman); I didn't have enough money; I wasn't acceptable to the right people, or that I never fit in with the "right groups of people," and I just didn't have the "right stuff," whatever that was. I am now in my mid-sixties and am finally over it.

Today I get it. I am enough, each and every day. Do I have it all together? No! But every day, I am doing the best I can with what I know in the moment. I am acceptable. I am all that I need and that God needs me to be. "All you have to do is *BE* who you are and that will be quite enough." Those were the words that were spoken to me very clearly in my head one day as I was walking back to my office from the Methodist Building, through the Capitol grounds, in Washington, D.C.

For the first five months of working in Washington, D.C. on Capitol Hill as a public policy advocate (lobbyist), I was literally asked by new colleagues all over the Hill, "Where did you come from? What are your credentials? Why are you here? What are your qualifications and why did they hire you?" I heard some form of these questions each and every day. These questions were so intimidating to me because, by the standards of my new colleagues, I did not have the "right" credentials. They were not consciously aware of this though, and my insecurity was shining through. By their standards, and my insecure thoughts, I should not have made it to that particular professional position alongside people who had earned Master's degrees or Ph.Ds. I think their biggest issue with me though was that I was new to the Hill and they did not easily invite new people into their world.

I had not yet come to understand that I had been given the best credentials and guidance of all that come from God. I had been given the gifts, experience, expertise, knowledge, and perceptions to do the job. I had been led to that position. My degree and experience was to be found in the life that I had lived, but I did not know that at the time because I was living with great internal fear.

To make matters worse, I discovered five months after being in my new work that my boss had been hiding mailings of meeting minutes, circulars, newsletters and all the information about one of my legislative issue responsibilities. I could not figure out why I wasn't getting the information that I had been told was sent to me. I was definitely in the dark when I went to meetings. You can imagine how incompetent I felt. It was awful. But I discovered what had been happening when one day I was led (by Spirit, I'm certain) to the desk drawer in which all of these papers had been crumpled and stuffed, evidently for many months. There were no words to describe my feelings of betrayal, but it did help to know that my feelings of insecurity had merit. My feelings were not without justification. Inside and outside of my office I was constantly being scrutinized and challenged. There was no comfort zone.

This experience helped me learn about how strong God's Light shines in the midst of the darkness. At this time in my life, I was led to reflect on the many times that I had been set up, abused without reason and not acknowledged for the Light that I carried of optimism, kindness, compassion and love. Years later I began to understand full well that God's Light is always stronger than the darkness. I have come to understand that Light is always threatening to the darkness of envy, jealousy, bigotry, discrimination, and unscrupulous behavior. Now I understand that sometimes all you have to do is exist, and that alone will be threatening to people who do not like who they are or do not like their particular circumstances. I also understand that some people do not want you to do a good job. Today I am glad that I was able to maintain optimism and faith through those trials.

As I reflect on this part of my story, I know that my internal fears were being reflected in my outer presence. Some people came after my insecurity because they needed to feel that they were better than me. They could tear me down in order to build themselves up. And I obliged them. I cried many tears privately. At the time I could not figure it out. I kept trying to provide what other people needed instead of functioning from the personal place of knowing what I needed in any given situation. I compared myself to others because I thought that, maybe, if I was like them, I would be accepted and the internal pain would cease.

Today I understand that I needed to be my very own authentic self and that would have been quite enough. In fact, being my authentic self would have allowed me to approve of myself instead of constantly being worried about whether I was doing my life "right" or not. Being my own authentic self would have provided the personal power that I needed (not power over someone or something) to act and behave in a place of love and not from fear. Being "sweet, sweet, sweet" was not what was called for. Standing in my own strength and power, with humility, was what was called for. Behaving from inner strength of the authentic me was what I needed to be able to do. But, for many years, I had no clue about how to be strong without being arrogant or being a know-it-all.

This book comes from much reflection and guidance that I have received from God on a daily basis of how to be the very best person that I can be. It also comes from experiences of getting through much pain and many challenges. Today I have the internal strength to function from the place of my authentic self. Today I live from a place of being centered and grounded in the knowledge of knowing who I am in a personal place of humility.

This book also comes from my work as a career and life coach for over thirty years. I have worked with many people and I know that I have been helpful to them. They have also been very helpful to me. I also know that I, personally, have not done the work with people all alone. God has been with me in every single client conversation and situation. I have come to understand how sacred each of our life experiences are, and I have been blessed to have had some of the best experiences of my life through the sharing that has taken place in my life and career coaching moments.

What clients helped me understand is that we all struggle as we face our fears in life. Few of us escape the struggle to be our best person as we live this life that we are privileged to live, no matter what our situation happens to be. Because clients have been willing to share their struggles with me, I have come to know that every person's life is sacred. If we open to the opportunity to do the required work, God will make a way for each and every one of us to move to a better and brighter future. We just have to be willing to understand the lessons that are placed before us. My experience is that when we ask for understanding, we will always receive the intuitive message. Be alert to the message that comes because it may not arrive when you expect it to or be what you were expecting it to be. We must pay attention and live symbolically by asking ourselves, "What must I learn from this experience of the moment?"

When we are at what feels like our lowest point in life and have no hope for a brighter future, we have to dig deep in order to rise up out of the ashes of life circumstances. If we can remind ourselves that this is where we are in this very moment and that tomorrow is another day, we can cling to the knowledge and understanding that God walks with us through our lives so that we can have a brighter tomorrow. We must have faith and trust that we are not alone. If we can keep the faith, we can make it over to the other side of the river.

It is my hope that you will take a look at your life, examine the gifts that you have been given, and think about the "messages" that have come through to you periodically. Celebrate yourself and gain the courage to live in your highest good each and every moment of your day.

Today what I know is that we do nothing alone and that getting through the rough waters of our life will most probably come at a high price. But, no matter what the challenges, we are supposed to learn something and then use it for a higher purpose, perhaps to help someone else make it through the rough waters of their life. With all of us doing our part, perhaps we can get through to the other side of the river with straight backs.

This book is an attempt to respond to the commitment and responsibility I have to God. I do this with gratitude because my back is still straight. I am grateful!

IN THE BEGINNING

It still amazes me that I have been able to move past being a victim in my life. Everyone's story and experience is different and requires different approaches to overcome the issues that get in the way of positive living. Life challenges happen most days. Sometimes we become tired of these challenges. However, I believe they are put in our lives for us to learn life lessons. Doing a one-hundred-and-eighty-degree turn in our lives, on any issue, requires a lot of thoughtfulness, intention to live better, and a lot of personal work. I have learned that when we replace our fear-based actions with an intention to live with love in our hearts, we can achieve a happier and better life. It really is that simple.

When we are intentional about living our life on purpose, this intention leads to greater life fulfillment and an opportunity to make a difference in the world. We can experience greater joy and happiness in our life as a result.

Crossing Rough Waters – Journey from Fear to Freedom, provides ideas that are meant to help you move forward so that you can attain the reality of living a positive, successful life. It contains my story of being a victim in my early life and doing the work to become victorious over a fear-based life. Taking the risk to change your life, not knowing where that change will lead, is a conscious decision that requires courage and tenacity. You will read about the challenging experiences that I wrestled with in order to make huge, significant changes in my life. I believe that if I can do it, so can you.

In the Beginning

Most of us have lived some portion of our lives entrapped by fear, pain, insecurity, or anger. For some people this can lead to a feeling of being a victim, and being a victim can become a way of life. That certainly was my truth for many years. The feelings of entrapment are not comfortable, but they are a known quantity. Living in this fear-based place provides a protective coping mechanism because we have not found positive ways to work through fear. We rationalize the current pain by maintaining the behaviors that got us through our past. Oftentimes, it feels safer to live the life that we know than to change.

Living this way becomes a vicious cycle that is not in our best interest. Peeking out from behind this fear-based protection is uncomfortable because we don't know what we will find. The truth is, we don't know how to release the fear, and it is not easy to claim our personal power in environments and relationships that have been designed to keep us powerless. We want a better, happier life; yet, life continues to give us lemons and we continue to learn to deal with them. We must consider new ways to approach the shackles that keep us chained to fear. When we have lived with fear for so long, it becomes difficult to muster the determination it takes to move forward.

As a life and career coach, I began to understand how critical it was to help clients identify their personal and professional God-given gifts and talents, as well as the skill sets they had developed. In past years, I rarely verbalized my coaching process with clients in a spiritual context; yet, it was from this vantage point that I did the work. My underlying, non-verbalized commitment for my clients was, "Ask and you shall receive." It was uncanny how often events would converge to help people realize and receive specifically what they had asked for. Because of these positive past experiences with many clients, today I am upfront in my private practice about coaching from a spiritual perspective.

I believe that every life is sacred and that every journey is a sacred adventure. Most of us don't have a clue about how to honor ourselves, much less see our lives as a sacred experience. It is important for us to do the work that resonates with the essence of who we are and then leave space for God to enter in to the process. We don't have all of the answers, and in my experience, the work that is needed does not reveal itself in a nice, neat package.

Discovering our life path is like putting puzzle pieces together. When we figure out one piece of the puzzle, we then have to figure out how we can best use this understanding. Then it is time to move on to the next piece. We ask ourselves how each part will fit into our whole life puzzle. It happens one piece at a time. When our gifts and talents are put into our own personal tool kit, the total package adds up to be the unique and wonderful individuals that we are.

It is my hope that *Crossing Rough Waters — Journey from Fear to Freedom* will help you to progress on your spiritual journey, while living a grounded life in the world. Often when we think of living a spiritual life, it conjures up an image of someone with an airy-fairy type of consciousness. That is not at all what I mean. What is important to me is this: To be a person who is guided by Spirit while living a very normal, grounded, and balanced life.

In order to emerge from being a victim to living a more fulfilling and exciting life, I learned that it was necessary to develop and live a strong faith in my daily life. This faith has given me the strength to allow my authentic self to shine. Focusing on thoughts and feelings of love in my heart and mind has been important in order to ground myself; yet, I don't believe the personal work ever ends, for there are always lessons to learn.

I hope this book will provide you with information to help you live a co-created, unique life with God, somewhere between spirituality and religion. If you follow a particular religion or belief system, please continue to do so. This book is not meant to change your beliefs; it is meant to help you think about the way you live on a moment-by-moment basis. Living our life requires *that* level of intention and consciousness. I believe that we all receive our own messages, often referred to as intuition, and I hope this book will inspire your own messages to come forward. More importantly, I hope that you will listen to your intuitive messages so that you may better serve and use your life in the world.

How to Get There from Here

Our primary goal for today is to be able to function from a place of strength by using our unique gifts and talents. It means living in the fullness of who we are and striving to be the compassionate, loving, witty, and intelligent people that we are. To do this, connecting with the best in ourselves is imperative. Courage and self-honesty are required. I know that it is possible to achieve this goal, for I am living proof.

When we are able to recognize and acknowledge the fear-based attitudes or behaviors that we have lived with, it becomes easier to release the fear and become victorious over that fear. Each of us will define living a successful and fulfilling life in different ways because we are individuals with unique life experiences. If we are to heal, we must address the reasons we have lived with fear, examine how we have coped with that fear, and then develop a plan to move past the fear.

I lived too many years of my life chained to fear. What I did not understand is that our fears feed on themselves. The more fear we have, the more what we don't want will come to us. We attract the feared beliefs and experiences. This can become a habit, and not one that serves us at all well. Each of us has the capacity to contribute either fear or love. In order to address and resolve the fear that we hold on to, we must face the issues surrounding our fear. In order to move from the disempowerment that fear creates, we must acknowledge the fears we have; only then can we create empowering attitudes and behaviors of love.

For me, being in a place of fear felt safe because that was all I knew. I could recognize that I was clinging to negative behaviors, but I had no clue how to move beyond the fear that seemed so protective. I had no idea what my strengths were, and I did not know how to find out. In my early adulthood I was caught in survival mode, just putting one foot in front of the other and working to pay for the necessities of life.

I often found myself in relationships with people who were unkind. I could not understand this because I prided myself on being a nice person. What I did not recognize is that I did not know how to honor myself in a non-ego-centered way. I saw what I considered to be huge egos all around me, and I did not want to behave like that. In time, I began to understand that I had to honor myself before anyone else would honor and respect me.

Each person must discover his or her own life path; this is one of the most challenging revelations for everyone. Oftentimes, life is revealed in paradox; yet, contradiction of painful experiences might hold our best opportunities. As an example, when I was being challenged each day on Capital Hill by people who seemingly questioned my every move, I questioned myself and that questioning reinforced my lack of confidence.

I began to gain more confidence when, intentionally, I reflected carefully on my past thoughts and words of insecurity; I changed my words. I began to be more reflective. I acknowledged and affirmed to myself that I moved through things more slowly than other people around me. At work I expressed my thoughts that we needed to listen to people all over the country instead of thinking that we, inside the Beltway, had all of the country's answers. This perspective was not popular, but I expressed it anyway. When I could finally stand up for my commitments, and what I knew to be true for me, I reflected more confidence than when I tried to accommodate the perspectives of other people.

Facing and then dissecting the painful aspects in our lives makes it easier to develop a plan for a more positive experience. Doing this work requires the deepest journey into personal truth-telling that you may ever experience. It is easy for us to speak negative beliefs about ourselves, but for some reason, we find it harder to acknowledge the positive truths. Acknowledging positive truths about ourselves is one of the most powerful gifts that we can own. Believe me, this work is required in order to develop a positive attitude about ourselves.

Our lives are strictly our own. We must live our own truths instead of what someone else thinks our truths ought to be. We all have our own answers. No one else can tell us how we "should" live or what decisions we "should" make. Ultimately, the decisions are ours to make. The "shoulds" that are sometimes spoken do not emanate from that positive place within us. They are often laced with fear and the expectations of other people in our life. "Shoulds" often do not come from the place of our very own personal authentic self.

As children, in our attempts to be accepted and loved, we tried to behave in ways that would receive approval from parents, siblings, teachers, friends, and others. We learned and modeled other people's rules and messages to us and we adopted their attitudes for "proper" behavior. Too often we were given negative messages about ourselves when we did not conform to their belief systems. As an adult, when we reflect on what we learned as children, it is important to take a barometer reading of what we learned to determine if those messages from our past fit in to our own unique lives. If they do not, we need to ask ourselves what changes we need to make.

The important thing is to take some and leave some behind. Don't throw the baby out with the bathwater and don't be rigid in your effort to do it "right." The world we live in as adults is so different from the world that we grew up in, and we too are different. This is why it is so important to take a personal reading of ourselves periodically to see if we like the unique person that we are becoming. As long as we live we are becoming who we are and we must be true to ourselves until our last breath. There is always room for growth and improvement. Consider what changes you need to make in the messages that you received from the past.

We are all on our very own life journey no matter who we are attached to or what our commitments are. Don't try to tell someone else who they are or what they "should" do. *Be reminded today* that you are God's gift in the world. It is extremely important to be reminded that you are on the planet today in order to live, as best as you can, the fullness of the gifts that you have been given. Be grateful for what is before you this day and do your best to live it fully.

I have learned that we are always where we are supposed to be, no matter what is going on at the moment. When I experienced tough times, I did not want to believe that I was where I was supposed to be, but I now recognize that I would not otherwise have learned the lessons that came with those times. I learned that everyone is doing his or her best, with what he or she has been given and knows at the moment. This truth allowed me to forgive and be more compassionate toward people I found difficult throughout my life. These people played an important role, though I was not always their focus; they were just trying to live their life with all that that meant for them. For my part, I learned lessons that were important for my own development.

Your personal story holds many keys to unlocking your greatest potential. It is a journey of self discovery. Truly getting to know the depth of who we are is one of the greatest challenges and joys in life. Be open to receiving your own intuitive messages, for they reflect many issues that come up. The question for us, over and over again, is what choice will we make? Our life journey contains the guidance for how God intends us to live. But the process is often tricky because, just when we thought that we had it all figured out, some new issue occurs that makes us rethink what we thought we knew. Being willing to wrestle with the new information and make changes is most important to our growth process.

Please do not compare your life with mine, but read my story as an example of one person's journey as a way of questioning and informing the thoughts you have about your own life experience. You can overcome adversity. Needless to say, I don't have all of the answers, but, over time, my challenges helped me make a positive turnaround to overcome the fear that I held. You might even discover some processes that work better for you than those that I have shared. Do what you need to do. This is your life, not mine or anyone else's, so do what works best for you.

In retrospect, I learned that experiencing the tough times in life helped me make a stronger spiritual connection. I am not so sure this could have happened without the challenges that I faced. It has all been a very powerful learning experience.

The Sacred Journey of Life

I have worked with many people over the years and I know that I have been helpful to them. In sharing the depth of who they are, they have been helpful to me as well. I know that I, personally, have not done the work with people all alone. God has been with me in every single client conversation and situation. I have come to understand how sacred each of our life experiences are, and I have been blessed to have had some of the best experiences of my life through the deep sharing that has taken place during life and career coaching moments.

My clients helped me understand that we all struggle with fear. Few of us totally escape the pain of our fears. We have to try to understand the lessons that are placed before us, and this is where faith, love, hope, and trust are important. Every time I have asked for understanding, I have received the intuitive message that would help me in a given situation. Be alert to the message that comes, because it may not be what you were expecting. Pay attention and live symbolically by asking yourself, "What can I learn from this particular experience?"

When we are at what feels like our lowest point in life and have no hope for a brighter future, we must dig deep in order to rise up out of the ashes of life circumstances. It is important to remind ourselves that this is where we are supposed to be right now: it is here that we are given the opportunity to stretch and grow. Cling to the knowledge and understanding that God walks with us through our lives so that we can have a brighter tomorrow by learning the lessons from challenging moments. We just need to have faith and trust that we are not alone. Maintaining faith helps us get to the other side of the turbulent river. Embracing our life as sacred is the faith we need for the journey.

The Road Is Long

What I know today is that we do nothing alone, and getting through the rapids of life will probably come at a high price. No matter what challenges we face, we can learn from them and use the experiences for a higher purpose. With all of us doing our part, perhaps we can all get to the other side of the river with straight backs.

This book is my attempt to respond to the commitment and responsibility that I have to God in gratitude, because I have crossed many rivers. Arriving at this place of understanding has been a long and arduous process. There were many years when I did not understand that faith in God would help to get me through life challenges. In fact, I was afraid to believe in God because I truly did not understand what faith meant. I could not see or touch a physical man, as had been depicted in church. I did not know how to apply a personal belief in this unseen being to my everyday life. Today I understand that there is an unseen force, a strong and powerful spirit. This force helps things happen that I am unable to achieve by myself. In fact, this force can move mountains and put things up before me that I would never have imagined possible. My life is now easier because of my understanding and belief in this Source of all that is.

My gratitude to this higher power leads me to understand that there is a divine order that I do not completely understand; the Great Mystery, as many American Indian people say. The existence of a divine order to things does not mean that we can sit back and do nothing. We must do our part, as we understand what we are to do. We have choices to make, and being open to receiving intuitive direction makes it easier.

If belief in God is not comfortable for you, please substitute what works for you and then proceed to grapple with the ideas that are drawn here. Throughout this book, I call the force that I believe in God; All That Is, Source, Great Spirit, the Universe, or Spirit. It is all the same to me. It is in this context that my thoughts are communicated.

What I Believe

I believe that we are not separate from God. I believe that we are God's instruments or messengers of peace, hope, compassion, and loving presence in the world. As we live our life, we are God's presence in the world. If we step back from being our best selves, we deny the power of the God who creates us.

There is nothing to fear. As we meet each other, we are meeting God in each encounter. Even people who are not behaving in ways that we appreciate are carrying God's spirit within. These people are sometimes nasty and exhibit much anger and make it difficult for us to be in their presence. They carry much fear and are unable to allow their best to shine through. They have erected walls of protection around themselves. Life events have cut them deeply, and these people can no longer trust their hearts to guide them in loving ways because they are afraid of being hurt.

People who appear to be living in fear provide opportunities for us to be compassionate toward them and speak truthfully about how their behavior affects us. I also find that when I don't take their words personally, sometimes there is a lesson for me to learn from my interaction with them. I try not to blame them but instead to speak about how I felt when I experienced their behavior or hurtful words.

I believe that life is a laboratory for our growth. We can learn about the purpose or plan for our life by walking through the maze of obstacles and challenges. In order to move forward in my life it was necessary to learn lessons from the challenges that I experienced. In doing this I became stronger. By having these experiences I developed personal values that reflected what I stood for, the integrity that I carried, and I could honor myself as an authentic person. But, none of this would have ever happened unless I was reflective and thoughtful about the clues that were placed before me.

Through this hard work, we are guided to our life purpose. When we arrive in this place of joy and fulfillment we are doing our special work in the world. We are truly then God's instruments in the world.

We Have Our Own Answers

Consider whether you like what your life experiences have been and if this reflection feels good. Self understanding allows us to look at our life honestly and to make necessary changes. If we can do this, we will not waste this life that has been given to us, and we will be better able to help others along the way.

We can help ourselves in our fast-paced world if we slow things down a bit in order to think things through instead of shooting from the hip. It isn't necessary to provide the right answer instantly when we are asked to do so. Good listening skills and reflection time can make all the difference. Take a break, walk around the block, take a deep breath, or go to the gym. Do whatever it takes. I believe we all have our own answers, and if we allow ourselves time to contemplate and reflect, then our intuition can kick in.

Take the time to ask for your own messages. What information pops into your head first? Discern whether the idea seems to truly fit the circumstance before you. If it does, write down the message and then contemplate it. Consider how you are going to step up, act on the message and follow through. It is important to consider whether the information you receive is appropriate to act upon when you think about all of the factors involved. Trust your perception and intuition. You will know.

When you decide to move forward, sometimes your action will be met with a positive response, and sometimes it will not be. Whatever the case, if you know in your heart that this is the proper course of action, have courage to follow through and carefully consider how and when you will present the new information.

Listen to Your Heart

Listening to our heart is essentially paying attention to the deep feelings and thoughts that we have. These deep messages are like listening to how God is leading or calling us. It is very important to slow down enough to listen to our heart's messages. If we follow this guidance, we will not be led astray.

If we pay attention to who we are individually and what our needs are, that will be quite enough. Don't try to tell someone else who they are or what they should do unless they ask for your thoughts or suggestions. It is quite enough just to focus personally on what we need to do in contemplating our own life.

I hope you will discover, as I have, that it is important to live fully from moment-to-moment, rather than in the past or in the future. Our past is meant to inform our present moment in the now of our lives. It is important for us to be grateful for what is present this day and to do our best to live it fully.

The future is ahead of us and does not exist at this moment. Living our best life now is individual and personal. No one else can tell us how to do it though they might try. You must remember this: we are not alone on our path. God is with us. When we believe this, our life is co-created and we are living with God in every manner of our life.

September Prayer

Spirit, thank you for this night
as the full moon blankets
the land where I live and
deep blue mystery above.

Thank you for the three deer
stepping like a whisper to nip late summer nectar
under old oaks outside my window
and for the song of crickets
constant until sleepy owls hoot
bringing the dawn sky.

Thank you, Spirit,
for the sacred breath of life
the ears I have to hear you
the eyes you have given me to see
and this tender heart of mine
to feel you forever around me.

Carla Riedel

Primary Messages in this Book

- We are not alone, for God's love is always with us.
- We are God's presence in the world. We are God's eyes, ears, voice, hands, and feet to serve in the world.
- There are no accidents or mistakes in life, just opportunities and victories to help learn lessons.
- Possibilities and opportunities are limitless.
- We learn from each other. We are all mirrors for each other.
- Difficulties can be the greatest teachers and provide the biggest lessons.
- It may take many years to process pain from experiences that occurred earlier in our life.
- We must forgive ourselves and others. Do not live in guilt.
- We live symbolically by asking what our life lessons of each moment are about, and then changing in order to reflect the lessons.
- Light is always more powerful than darkness.
- We must be mindful of the decisions and choices that we make. Everything that happens in life is bigger than it appears because it often impacts more than the decision-maker.
- The need for our service in the world is great.
- We must be kind to ourselves; then be kind to everyone and everything.
- We can have the courage to replace fear with love in every moment that we feel fearful.
- We are God's gift in the world. We must live our life fully.
- Life is a ceremony of gratitude.

Love Is the New Religion
(A Spiritual Conspiracy)

On the surface of the world right now there is war and
violence and things seem dark.
But calmly and quietly at the same time something else is
happening underground.
An inner revolution is taking place and certain individuals
are being called to a higher Light. It is a silent revolution.
From the inside out. From the ground up.
This is a Global operation. A Spiritual Conspiracy.
There are sleeper cells in every nation on the planet.
You won't see us on the T.V. You won't read about us in the
newspaper. You won't hear about us on the radio.
We don't wear any uniform.
We come in all shapes and sizes, colors and styles.
Most of us work anonymously.
We are quietly working behind the scenes in every country
and culture of the world, cities big and small, mountains and
valleys, in farms and villages, tribes and remote islands.
You could pass by one of us on the street
and not even notice. We go undercover.
We remain behind the scenes. It is of no concern to us who
takes the final credit but simply that the work gets done.
Occasionally we spot each other on the street.
We give a quiet nod and continue on our way. During the day
many of us pretend we have normal jobs.

But behind the false storefronts at night is where the
real work takes place.

Some call us the Conscious Army. We are slowly creating a
new world with the power of our minds and hearts.

We follow, with passion and joy. Our orders come from the
Central Spiritual Intelligence.

We are dropping soft, secret love bombs
when no one is looking:

Poems ~ Hugs ~ Music ~ Photography ~ Movies ~ Kind
words ~ Smiles ~ Meditation and Prayer ~ Dance ~ Social
Activism ~ Websites ~ Blogs ~ Random acts of kindness…

We each express ourselves in our unique ways with our
unique gifts and talents.

"Be the change you want to see in the world."

That is the motto that fills our hearts.

We know it is the only way real transformation takes place.

We know that quietly and humbly we have the power of all
the oceans combined.

Our work is slow and meticulous like the formation of
mountains. It is not even visible at first glance, and yet, with
it entire tectonic plates shall be moved in the centuries to
come. Love is the new religion of the 21st century.

You don't have to be a highly educated person or have any
exceptional knowledge to understand.

It comes from the intelligence of the heart embedded in the
timeless evolutionary pulse of all human beings.

In the Beginning

Be the change you want to see in the world.

Nobody else can do it for you.

We are now recruiting!

Perhaps you will join us, or you already have.

All are welcome.

The door is open.

Reprinted with permission by
Brian Piergrossi THE BIG GLOW
www.thebigglow.com

A Daily Mantra for your Journey

To help you be victorious on a daily basis, use this powerful mantra and consider what it means for you: *Be Reminded Today.* When I recite this mantra, I am reminded to live with love in my heart. I am reminded to release any fears that I might have. By reminding ourselves that we are God's gift in the world, we are helped to take charge of ourselves in order to serve the higher good. We are God's instrument in the world. Our words speak the words that God is saying through us. Our actions act out what God intends to be done in the world. The energy we carry permeates the room and the world at large and is the energy that can change and impact attitudes and behaviors all around us. We are here to live our best life with grace, love, responsibility, and humility. The possibilities are limitless.

Be Reminded Today

Be reminded today that we are God's gift in the world
Be reminded today as you shower and dress for the day
Be reminded today as you get your child ready for school
Be reminded today as you have breakfast
Be reminded today as you pass another person on the street
Be reminded today in supermarket conversations
Be reminded today as you develop and work on important projects
Be reminded today in a mall or speaking with a cashier
Be reminded today as you encounter an angry person

In the Beginning

Be reminded today as you hug your pet
Be reminded today as you look at a tree, or a rock, or water
Be reminded today in airplanes, busses, trains or car
Be reminded today as you meditate and pray

Sarah Payne, 8 months

MY STORY

I had difficult experiences with my parents. I know that I stuffed a lot inside about what happened during my childhood. Dottie, my friend since the fourth grade, has helped me see some of the experiences that I had buried because they were too painful to remember. I couldn't even remember some of the fun events, because they were too few and far between the difficult times. But now I am past all of that. I have developed an understanding of why these times were so difficult. I think that I have learned many of the lessons that I was supposed to learn in order to become more mature and to be a person who carries wisdom rather than pain. At the same time, I understand that there are more experiences to come into my life from which I can learn.

Today, I have so much gratitude in my heart for the experiences that I had with my parents and brothers. Without them, I would certainly not have learned the life lessons I did, nor would I have become the person that I am today. From this perspective, I am able to share the difficulties and challenges that I experienced, because I do so with love in my heart and with the intention that my experiences may be helpful to someone else.

Mainly, I have learned that each of us have our own lessons in life, my parents and brothers included. I have forgiven myself for my criticism of them and I have forgiven them for all of the difficult times that we experienced together. Today I know that we each had our own lessons to learn and those lessons were expressed in different ways. We played out our parts in each other's life scenarios so that, individually, we could learn what we needed to learn. I have learned how important it is for each of us to tell our stories truthfully, at least, to ourselves, so that we can learn, grow, heal, and move toward more positive endeavors in our lives. The primary goal in sharing my story is to help each person who reads it to delve into his or her own story and bring up the nuggets of truth that will help the healing process take place.

The social, economic, and geographic context in which our lives take place is important to consider. That said, American society also played a part in the difficulties of my family. Racism was alive and well and it greatly affected us on a personal level. Economic conditions also contributed in large measure to the challenges that my family faced. When I reflect on those times, I realize that America has come a long way, but there is still a long way to go to repair, heal, and reverse the disparities that are evident in our country today. Racism and poverty played a huge part in the abusive environment that I experienced as a child. Unfortunately, neither condition has gone away.

As people meet each other, we must consider our life stories and the impact of the conditions of society on each other's lives. Remember, the face that we see represents a mask of a much larger story. We need to get to know each other in real ways and allow ourselves the opportunity to share our love with each other with greater compassion and non-judgment. If we could do that, the world would be a much better place for us to live.

Hopefully, by reflecting on your own life as you read my story, you will gain insights from your experiences that will provide some guidance for your future. It is time now for us to heal ourselves from being a victim. It is time for us to become the victorious people that we are capable of being. It is time for us to do the work that is required to release us from any pain that we felt from being in our families of origin, or from society's ills, so that we can live the sacred life that is intended for each of us.

My growing up years

I was born in Berkeley, California where, when I was very young, we lived in a rooming house apartment. My brother, John, was a little baby and I must have been two or three years old. I remember this place because we had to share one bathroom with other tenants in this rooming house. Our apartment was very crowded, and it was hard on all of us. I don't remember being able to run around and play. I always had to be quiet. I remember sounds more than sights in this place because the noise made it difficult to sleep at night.

After living at the rooming house, we lived in Altamont, California, near San Jose. For a short time, my father repaired the rails with other workmen and we lived in one of the small houses owned by the railroad. During that time, Altamont was a rural community with only a few houses and some farms. I used to watch my mother iron clothes with an iron that was heated atop the stove. One day I was outside and I heard the sound of animals coming my way. It was a herd of cows, and I had never seen cows before. The cows were big and seemed to be moving very fast. I thought they were coming after me. I ran inside, shouting to my mother that big animals were coming to get me. I was scared and excited. She explained that they were cows and that they wouldn't harm me. I can still remember shaking with fear. Before I knew it, they were gone, thank goodness.

Not long after that experience, we moved to Redwood City, California. My most vivid memory from there involved a neighbor's wandering chicken. Evidently my father had asked the neighbor to keep his chickens in his own yard. The owner of the chickens must not have paid attention to my father's requests. One day a chicken pecked chicken feed right up to our front door. My father grabbed the chicken, and I could hear it squawking as he killed it. I yelled at the top of my lungs, "Daddy, what are you doing with that chicken?" "Shut up," he shouted.

The next thing I remember is that my mother removed the feathers from the chicken, cooked it, and served it for our dinner that night. My parents laughed about how the chickens did not come into our yard anymore. It's funny what one remembers from being a toddler.

From Redwood City, we moved to the housing projects in Richmond, California in the late 1940s. My mother got up each morning around 4:00 AM to prepare for her workday in San Francisco. Preparation meant getting three young children ready for school. She had to make sure that we were dressed and fed, make our lunches, and take us to a babysitter who lived downstairs in our building. I cannot imagine how she felt about having to leave us with this woman. The sitter was not as responsible as our own mother would have been with us, but our mother had no choice because she had to go to work. She rode the ferry across the San Francisco Bay each morning. There was no road or rail connection from the East Bay to San Francisco at that time.

My mother had to trust that this woman would make certain that we safely made our long trek to the school-bus stop each weekday. The sitter was usually entertaining men and paid little attention to the three of us children. Her only goal was to collect the money from our parents. Neither of our parents could be there to make sure that we got to or from school safely. My father worked in the shipyards and his workday began before daybreak. It must have been so hard for my parents.

Those housing projects were perilous places for the three of us children. I can still remember the playground. There were swings and slides that had lots of sand on the ground underneath. But what I remember most is that there was a boy named

Butch who made it his business to terrorize us. The three of us were peace-loving children and just wanted to play and have fun. But Butch made that impossible. He taunted us and tried to pick fights with us, but we were afraid to fight back.

At the end of each building there were huge incinerators for tenants to burn paper and cardboard or other disposable materials. On one particular day, the fire was blazing in the incinerator that was near our building. Butch came after us and insisted that John, my younger brother, get in the incinerator with the fire blazing. He wanted John to burn up. I ran to get my father, but my Dad made me go back outside and told me that there were three of us and we should beat Butch up. Now, mind you, we were all under the ages of 6 years old and we were not fighting children. I could not believe that my father wasn't going to come to our rescue. I ran back outside and shouted to John not to get in the incinerator and that we should run for our lives. We ran and ran. Finally, Butch went away and found someone else to bully. That place always seemed to hold such peril for us children. Other children always seemed to want to fight too. We just wanted to play and have fun. The only real safe place for us was inside our apartment.

We moved from those Richmond housing projects after what could have been a fatal experience for my father. One morning a bullet whizzed through our apartment and just missed his head as he was shaving. That incident precipitated our sudden move to Del Paso Heights, outside of Sacramento.

The rental house my parents were waiting to move us into was not yet ready when we arrived. As a result, the five of us lived in our car for a couple of days at Southside Park in Sacramento. My parents tried to make it seem like an adventure, serving us Cheerios and Wheaties, pouring milk into the small individual boxes for breakfast, and then letting us out of the car to play on the playground. I cannot begin to imagine how vulnerable my parents must have felt during that time of our lives. Those experiences are indelibly etched in my memory and have sensitized me to the threats that homeless families face in today's society.

The house that we had been waiting for was finally ready. When I awakened the first morning that we lived in Del Paso Heights, I was surprised that I could see cracks of daylight showing through the walls next to my bed. There was no insulation and the wallboard wasn't well positioned.

That first winter was pretty cold, but the experience in this house spurred my parents to save enough money, and get a loan, so that they could buy a vacant lot across the street and have a small house built. By the time we moved into our own house, my third brother had been born, making four children in our family. We all lived in this house with two bedrooms and one bath until my parents could manage to have an additional bedroom added on for my brothers. The additional bedroom was built at the end of the house.

I was given the small bedroom where the four of us children

had been sleeping in bunk beds. But the only way in and out of the boys' bedroom to the rest of the house was through my bedroom. Needless to say, there was always somebody going through my bedroom. This was our home until I graduated from high school when we moved into town.

These were challenging years for my parents as they tried to keep it together for a family of six. My mother continued to work outside the home and, because she was very competent and light-complexioned, she did not have trouble getting work nor did she experience the kind of harassment that my dad did. Her skin color and gender were not a threat to white America.

My mother was the parent who provided the economic stability in our family, though my father also worked. In retrospect, I feel sorry for the way racial conditions in America affected my parents. Their role reversal was not intentional or by design; it resulted from necessity. My mother was able to keep jobs; my father was often harassed by co-workers, which made his employment more unstable. He could not tolerate the racial insults, and, frankly, I totally understand his position.

My mother was a beautiful and poised woman who, I am certain, often experienced the threat of men trying to seduce her. She developed a stern public exterior and did not exude much warmth to strangers. She could verbally lash out at anyone and chew them up in a heartbeat. If she didn't like you, she let you know it. Obviously, this kept people at a distance, so it was difficult to see and experience her heart. For those people she did like, she could be the most loving, thoughtful, and considerate person imaginable.

From my perspective today, I have a greater understanding and compassion for my parents. I grew up in an economically poor, semi-rural community outside of Sacramento, but I did not know at the time that this was the way our community was socially identified. There were no sidewalks or street lights. It was a place where people were just trying to make it.

I was born the year after World War II ended. Our country was still in the throes of depression, and times were hard for everyone. So much of my relationship with my parents was emotionally abusive and almost schizophrenic, sending a message of, *Yes, I love you, but I'll beat you senseless (physically and emotionally) for your own good.* I believe that many people of my generation had that experience. *I won't protect you against meanness from other children or adults because the world isn't a nice place,* was the message my parents gave me. *You have to become tough and learn how to protect yourself. You have to fight for yourself. Don't expect us to be there for you.*

Though there were many challenges in my family, my parents insisted that their children not behave as many of the other children did in our neighborhood. We had to toe the mark. This was uncomfortable for me because I wanted desperately to be accepted and to make friends among the neighborhood children. Our mother insisted that we call her "mother" instead of "mama". My parents were strict and enforced rules on me and my brothers from a young age. We were not allowed to speak street slang in our house, so it got to be too much trouble to be "hip" on the street and then be proper in our home. We were truly out of step with most of our classmates. Today I realize that this was not a bad thing. We all grew up knowing how to converse with everyone and we knew how to behave in various situations.

We had very few opportunities to develop friendships outside of school because my parents took us to visit my great aunt in Berkeley or my grandparents in East Palo Alto, two to three weekends out of each month. There was no time to develop friendships or to engage in extra-curricular activities in our community during the weekends.

My brothers and I were taught proper etiquette and manners, and we were expected to live by these values. This was not unusual for the time but, in our neighborhood, most children were not raised with the strict rules that my parents expected us to follow. We did not dare break any of our parents' rules because punishment in our house was harsh. Enforcement of their rules seemed to become very strict once we moved to Del Paso Heights. My siblings and I lived with great fear all of the time.

In our home, my parents held us hostage at the dinner table every evening – at least, that is what it felt like - talking about world events of the time. They had daily conversations about world conditions that could have been heard in family homes of university professors. My parents were well-read and intelligent. They communicated their politics and values about the world with each other, yet they did not talk with us directly about any of this. They did not engage us in conversation, and they did not really want to know how our day at school had gone. We were to sit there quietly and eat our meal, and speak only when spoken to. When we were spoken to, our responses had to be, "Yes, Mother," or "Yes, Daddy." That was it. Other adults praised my parents for having such well-mannered children.

My friend Dottie said that the few times she came to our home for a meal, it was like visiting a foreign land. Nobody else's parents in our neighborhood had conversations like my parents, talking about Mahatma Gandhi, Haile Selasse, or Chiang Kai-shek, to name but a few. My coping mechanism was to try to "make nice" all of the time so that my parents would know that I was their good little girl and that I was paying attention to them.

Difficult Relationship With My Father

My brothers and I lived in fear that we would incur our father's instant wrath if we made one wrong move. Every day after we moved to Del Paso Heights, my father beat us, sometimes multiple times during the day. We were just children, and there was no way that we could ever be perfect. No one knew about the beatings except our next-door neighbors who heard us crying and yelling in pain.

To my dismay, there was nothing I could do to head off the beatings. I remember once when I was about eight or nine years old I was lying in my bed awake very early in the morning. I was sobbing quietly under the covers and pleading with God to please help me be a good little girl today. I asked for God's help because I did not want to get a beating that day. It hurt so badly, and it made me feel so awful inside. I just did not know what to do. I continued to try to be good, but to no avail.

My father had turned into a rage-aholic and would release his unchecked anger on us at the drop of a hat. His belt would come off in a flash and would find its intended victim in a heartbeat. If one of us children was the focus of his wrath and the belt, we all got it. His belief was that the others should have stopped the guilty one, which would have kept us all from getting in trouble. The beatings took place every day until I was nearly thirteen years old. That was when I got my period, and my father stopped beating me, but his yelling and screaming rages persisted. He never raged against my mother; he only showed love and affection toward her.

His frustration with his life came out in other ways too that were challenging to live with.

My father had a hoarding disorder and collected things but never threw anything away. If someone had taken a photo of our yard in Del Paso Heights, at any given time, there would have been three to five cars in front of our house at any given time, all in various stages of disrepair. There was always a lot of junk in our yard. Our detached garage was loaded to the gills with old televisions, radios, speakers, and tubes. Inside the house wasn't much better. Huge speakers, radios, and televisions from the neighborhood sat in our living room for my father to repair. His customers waited several weeks for their possessions to be returned.

Their televisions, and radios would sit on the piano bench or on the coffee table or wherever there was room available. Always present were loads of books and magazines stacked up in the living room. It was a chaotic mess, and it was always that way.

Even when we finally moved to a larger house in town, it wasn't long before my father's stuff was everywhere all over again. I especially remember having piles of stuff almost to the ceiling around three sides of our dining room table, leaving little space for a family of six to eat meals. My mother complained about the mess and sometimes would throw my Dad's stuff away. But it didn't matter, because, in very short order, it would be replaced with more stuff.

Today I find it easier to understand my father's behavior because he lived daily with racism and disappointment in his life. He was a very dark-complexioned proud black man who was subjected to discrimination and bigotry. He was one of the most intelligent men I have ever known. He read everything

54

that he could get his hands on.

My father's frustration with the racial and financial conditions in America prevented him from taking good economic care of his family and this contributed to his rage. On a daily basis, I heard him talk about Caucasian people as "the Man." Most of his daily conversations with us were about the discriminatory practices and controlling behavior that white America had over black America. He experienced it daily.

Deep down, my father was a very loving man, but he lived a hard life and made life difficult for his children because we were the only ones that he had any degree of power over. As a child, there was nothing I could do to get away from his anger. Although, to the outside world, we seemed to get along well together like a "normal" family, whatever that is.

I later learned that my grandmother was not married at the time of my father's birth. He must have heard that he was a "bastard child" all of his life because that is the message about himself that he took to his grave. His rage stemmed from the very beginning of his life. He was born in 1916 and was not baptized in the Black church in Missouri (and baptism was a big deal in the Black family church) because he was considered to be a bastard child. In the eyes of the church, according to my father, that meant God could not accept him into the fold. My father asked to be baptized when he was more than sixty years old in a neighborhood Lutheran church in Sacramento. Knowing this part of his story helped me forgive his behavior toward me and my brothers when we were children. It also helped me forgive him that when I was thirty-five years old he asked for my forgiveness. *"I am asking for your forgiveness for the many times that I beat you and your brothers,"* he said. *"I am aware that it is only because of your ability to forgive me that I even have a relationship with you today. I am very grateful, and I love you very much."* Even if I had not understood what a difficult life he had, those loving words were all I needed. They were an incredible gift and I will always be grateful to him for coming to terms with himself and his behavior and then having the courage to share that moment with me.

As I was growing up, l saw that my father was very intelligent, had a wonderful singing voice, exposed us to all genres of music on his hi-fi, and could occasionally be funny. Unfortunately, he did not know how to have fun with his children. Even though it was a difficult time for him, I am grateful that he did not leave us. Although his presence was difficult for me, he provided a kind of stability to the family unit that I am grateful we had.

I realized through the years that he tried and tried to overcome the challenges that he faced and he really tried to provide for his family as best as he could. When I reflect on those times, I realize that he must have suffered from depression about being unemployed and all of the other challenges that he could do little about.

I remember that when I was in high school, he finally got a job working for the County of Sacramento as a grave digger.

It was a horrible experience for him. One day, soon after he began his new job, he came home shaking all over. He told us that the wooden box that he was burying had fallen apart, and the body parts had come out all over the ground. He had to put the box back together and put the person's parts back inside. I cannot even begin to imagine what this must have been like for him.

From that day forward, I held such compassion in my heart for him and I forgave him for all of the pain and suffering that he had inflicted on me. I held him in the highest regard possible. He quit the grave digging job soon after the coffin fell apart, thank goodness. After that experience, it was very hard for my father to function. I think he suffered from post-traumatic stress syndrome, but we were not aware of such a diagnosis during that time. It took him a long time to recover from that work experience.

Soon after that, our family moved into town and my father was hired for the second time by the County of Sacramento; this time as an electrician, a job that he held until he retired. He loved his work, mainly because he had his own county truck and he had the freedom to make electrical repairs without having someone looking over his shoulder. All they wanted to know was whether or not the repair had been done satisfactorily. He always did a good job.

A funny story I remember about my father was when he gave me a car to drive. I had been working for a year at the Sacramento County Hospital when I began attending classes at Sacramento State College part-time. I needed to be able to get myself to and from both places, which were many miles apart. The car that my dad gave me to drive was a stick-shift Studebaker that did not have first gear or reverse. Early in my attendance at Sacramento State College, I figured out that I had to get to the campus very early in the morning, no matter what time my classes began, because there were only two parking spaces on the entire campus that had even the slightest bit of an incline. Due to the fact that I could not put the car in reverse, in order to get out of the space I had to bump up against the parking block of the space, keep my foot pressed down on the clutch and allow the car to roll back out of the space and then proceed to move forward. It required very tricky maneuvering.

If I drove to downtown Sacramento, the only parking spaces I could safely use were the ones at the beginning of the block so that I could pull into them and simply drive forward when I left the parking space. There was no parallel parking option for me in this car. Eventually, second gear went out and that was all she wrote. The interesting thing was that my father was able to repair cars, but procrastination kept him from ever fixing mine. By the time second gear went out in my car, I decided to go out and buy a 1963 Volkswagen bug. Since my father was working full-time, my thought was that our family no longer needed my financial contribution. I did not ask for permission or approval; I just did it. Needless to say, my father was not happy with me. When I reflect back on that time, I realize that purchasing my own car must have felt like a slap in the face to him.

The experience of driving cars that were in various stages of disrepair informed my knowledge about driving any vehicle. I can hear or feel the slightest problem in my car and have a sense of what is needed to bring it back to good driving condition. I can drive just about any vehicle of any configuration – because I drove cars that were not in the best repair when I was younger. Today I see it as a blessing, and really I have my father to thank for this instinct that I developed with cars.

Experiences with my mother

During my childhood I had no clue that there was a problem with my mother. She was someone that I admired and had placed on a pedestal. I emulated the way she walked and carried herself. She was beautiful and everyone looked at her with great respect. After all, my father was the one who had beaten us, and he was the one who did not seem to be engaged in the financial maintenance of the family on a regular basis.

All of the things my mother had said about men seemed to be true from my experience with my father. However, it wasn't until my teenage years that I began to understand how emotionally abusive my mother was toward me; yet the abuse didn't seem real because it wasn't something that I could physically feel. I was also frightened and insecure and could not bring myself to question her actions. What's more, questioning my mother would not have been the polite thing to do.

My mother taught me that I needed to learn the ways of manipulation in order to be feminine, for this is what women did during those years. Of course I reject this behavior today because manipulation gets in the way of real and honest relationships. My mother said that I could not really have or be what I wanted because my desires should always come last. She was very critical of me, though she thought she was teaching me.

In my mother's eyes all men were irresponsible, uncaring, insensitive, and of little worth. It was very confusing to me though because I always heard my mother call my father 'honey.' They kissed each other often and I frequently saw them holding hands. They were very affectionate toward each other and seemed to treat each other with love and consideration during the years that I lived with them. Yet, on a daily basis, she used my father as her example to me about how worthless men were. Since my father had difficulty keeping a job and because he had an eruptive temper her messages made sense, though they were somewhat confusing to me as an adolescent girl.

My father had several short-term jobs during my childhood. He would get a new job and would go out to work, or so I thought. My mother would be waiting for his paycheck, but he didn't bring it home. What I didn't know, until my adult years, was that he was often called "nigger", or insulted in some demeaning way, and he would become very angry and walk off the job. Or he would say something insulting back to his boss and be fired immediately. His resulting periodic unemployment only fed my mother's negative attitude about men and provided fodder for her to use in her attempts to brainwash me. In my first marriage, if I was having a conversation with my husband, my mother would go stand behind him and her facial expressions would approve or disapprove of whatever I was saying or doing. I was so insecure that I would gasp if she gave me disapproving frowns. I never got used to that and I never did confront her about it.

After I had been nursing my baby son for about six months, my mother asked how long I intended to "keep doing that." I told her that I did not know and that I would continue to do it as long as possible. Her response was that it was time to stop because it was for my baby's health, not my enjoyment. I told her that I had not decided when we would stop. She expressed anger and disgust. The very next day, my son stopped nursing. I could not believe that. That was when I understood that she had powers that I did not understand and it was frightening to me, but I did not know what to do about it.

Over time I began to understand how my mother manipulated relationships with my brothers and other family members and friends against me. I would discover untruths that she had told about me and lies about other people that she knew would hurt me.

At one point, she told me that it didn't matter to her that I was her daughter because my sister-in-law was more of a daughter to her than I was. I was deeply hurt and shocked by that statement. I did not ever have jealousy about the relationships she had with daughters-in-law, however I was disturbed that she would even think to tell me something like that. That statement fed my insecurity and made me wonder whether there was more that I needed to do or be as her daughter. I just could not figure it out. Finally, I decided to just forget it because there was nothing that I could do to change my relationship with her. It was just one more time that she had seemed to intentionally hurt me.

One thing that made my mother's behavior so difficult to absorb was that no one ever wants to believe that her mother is unkind toward her. I didn't want to believe what was happening so I looked for different explanations. She could also be wonderful toward me. She taught me to sew, knit, and crochet. We had fun times together in fabric stores. Her behavior was confusing and made me question myself. Was I imagining the lies? Was I inventing the manipulative behaviors? It didn't make sense, and I questioned myself and was ashamed for even questioning my mother's motives.

Then she would do something else that helped me see that I

had actually perceived the truth accurately. I never had the courage to question her directly. Being her daughter was quite an interesting and challenging experience. No one would ever have believed the story of my difficult relationship with my mother because the experiences that I had with her were not what she displayed publicly. She was careful to treat me well in front of friends and even my brothers. Occasionally, though, she would slip and do something unkind to me in front of my father, but he never confronted her in front of me; he would just move away from the situation at hand.

When I lived in the Washington, D. C. area, I called my parents regularly and the duration of those conversations were controlled by my mother. She controlled whether or not I could speak with my father. She limited how much conversation she and I had together. Those conversations were often laced with nasty attacks and untrue, hurtful comments. When I shared, out of excitement, some of the positive experiences that I was having in my professional life, she told me that I was being very egotistical and that I should watch that. She knew what would upset me and her attacks were relentless. Every conversation we had left me in tears. I could not understand why she was doing this. In time, I decided not to share any personal information with her. My input into the conversations became more about the weather or our pets, but nothing personal.

After many years of this kind of behavior toward me, I thought that perhaps there was something terribly wrong. I began to realize that I could tell by her tone what kind of conversation we were going to have. When the tone was harsh and short, she would make cutting and cruel remarks. I decided not to take it personally anymore. I made certain that those conversations with her were brief. When her tone was inviting and friendly, I stayed on the phone longer and we then seemed to have pleasant conversations. I truly began to wonder whether she had some form of multiple personality disorder because that was what I experienced from her. In any case, I definitely decided that I needed to protect myself by monitoring how I engaged with her.

In a recent visit, before she passed away, my husband Ed and I traveled to Sacramento to see my parents. When we arrived there, the house was filthy and in total disarray. My younger brother was living with them at the time. I was very disturbed by what I saw. After Ed and I left, I called the brother who lived with them and my other brother who lived out of state and asked if we could have a family meeting because I was very concerned about whether our parents were able to continue to care for themselves. I thought a solution to their maintenance might be finding someone to help them take care of the home so that they could continue to live there. My concern was that if either of them became ill and needed to have an ambulance come for them, it would be noticed that their home was not in good condition and they might be removed to a facility of some kind. Neither of my brothers wanted to meet with me to talk about what we could do to be helpful. After visiting my parents, Ed and I left to visit a friend in the Bay Area. Taking a couple of days to think about it, I told Ed that I wanted to go back and see them one more time before we returned to our home in the East. When we arrived at my parent's home, my mother and father were sitting on the sofa, hands locked tightly together, with the TV blaring so that we could not really hear each other, and they were not very welcoming, in general. My brother who lived with them was standing behind them watching the whole scene.

It felt very much like they were all three guarding themselves against us. Intuitively, I realized that my brother had told them something that made them afraid. In those two days that I had been gone, the house had been cleaned and everything was put away. They were making a statement. *You are not welcome here and we want you to leave.* I knew that my father was not of that mind, but, my mother and brother definitely were. A few years later, after my father had passed away, I went to visit my mother. She asked whether I had wanted to put her and my father in a nursing home. That question did not surprise me. I told her, "no." And I further went on to say that, "you have all told so many lies about me and made up things that I have said. None of it is true, and none of you believe that I have love for you in my heart, or that I care about what happens to you." She had nothing to say to that, but that was one time when I told her my truth.

Understanding and acknowledging the truth about my relationship with my mother was important to my own development. I never had the nerve to question her directly about her feelings toward me; yet, I feel fairly certain that she would have denied her behavior. I just sucked it up and chose to be as loving as possible in our toxic relationship. Once I received counseling advice to "divorce" myself from her, but I could not do that. She was my mother. Years earlier, one of her offspring, my brother, had already divorced her and later committed suicide.

What I could do was acknowledge the truth of my experience with her. Once I did that, I seemed to become stronger. I refused to become weakened by her untruths and unfounded accusations. When I finally acknowledged her behavior, intuitive messages came to me saying that her behavior wasn't normal. I realized that she had sometimes seemed somewhat schizophrenic or paranoid in her relationship with me, but, there did not seem to be anything that I could do about it that would have made a difference. As I saw it, my biggest challenge was to not lose myself in the toxicity of it all, and it was important to be able to tell myself my truth of what I knew was in my heart. And it greatly helped that I lived on the other side of the country.

Finally, I could stop taking her behavior personally. I realized that her behavior toward me stemmed from something deeper, and I truly understood that my mother's life had been difficult. Her own life was not as she had hoped it would be. Many times she had told me that she did not like her life and that if she could do it over, she would not have gotten married or had children. As her daughter, that was difficult to hear because, children, even adult children, think that somehow they have caused their parents' pain.

Since my mother's death in 2006, I have tried to make sense of this very toxic relationship. I have asked God, *What was that about?* As a young adult, I tried to make sense of it by saying, *We had a very dysfunctional family.* I thought our family was the only one in the world that was dysfunctional and I thought that I was the only person in the world who had experiences with their family like I did. Obviously, that wasn't true, but I didn't know it at the time.

A year after my mother died, I decided to visit a reputable psychic who was able to connect with my mother on the other side. The unprompted message from my mother was that she was very sorry for all of the pain and suffering she had caused me. During her lifetime, she was never able to apologize to me for anything that she said or did. Toward the end of her life, the closest she came was saying that she was sorry that I had had a difficult childhood.

From her perspective, everyone else was to blame for whatever unpleasant situation occurred. She further communicated in this psychic reading that she had had a very difficult and painful life and she thought she was preparing me for "the tough, cruel world." Before the session ended, she apologized to me, again, for the way she treated me.

Needless to say, I am grateful for this message of apology and explanation. Though the experiences were extremely difficult, I am glad that I finally received this message from her. Even after her death, it was salve for my heart and soul. This communication helped me to be able to release a lot of pain. Today, I get it. I realize that her life was difficult and that she was doing the best she could.

About three years before her death, I learned one of my mother's most profound secrets. One of the women in our family that she had always referred to as her cousin was, in reality, her birth mother. My mother denied this fact to me, though I am certain that she knew the truth. Now I truly understand the pain that she had lived with.

The Family Secret

In 1999, I learned that the woman whom I had always thought of as Cousin Rosa was actually my maternal grandmother. This was only one of many revelations about my mother's family that came to light at that time. My mother did not acknowledge Rosa as her mother, but my Grandma Rosa has spoken to me through the reputable psychic whom I mentioned earlier and told me, "Of course you are my blood."

My mother was raised by Agnes and Joseph Rowe. Agnes died when I was a month old, so I never knew her, but she is the person whom my mother loved and honored as her mother and so do I. However, since I never knew a maternal grandmother, I found real solace in connecting to Grandma Rosa. She was an incredible woman. Other family members said that she was strong, steady, supportive, and had a heart of gold. I saw her a few times in my adulthood, but she never talked much. I had the feeling that she was a shy person, and now I understand why she shied away from me.

As a child, I never knew most of my mother's people in the mid-west. I would hear about them, but I only met one couple who came to visit us in Del Paso Heights from Detroit. It wasn't until I was in my mid-thirties that I went to my first family reunion for the Traylors, my mother's side of the family. I had been living in the Washington, D.C. area at that time. I will never ever forget the first day of the reunion when I saw one of the few cousins I knew from the San Francisco Bay Area. We laughed about how we had to come all the way to Philadelphia to see each other. When we walked into the building where the gathering was being held, we saw three old men sitting on a bench yakking it up with each other. One gentleman looked up and asked me, "Who are you? What line are you on? Who are your people?"

I really didn't know. All I could say was that my grandfather was Joe Traylor. What I had not realized is that Joseph was a name often used in the family. I could see the wheels turning in his head as he tried to figure out what "line" I descended from. I then remembered that my grandfather had changed his last name to Rowe — another family name. I told these men that my grandfather had moved to California to escape the vigilantes who were hunting him down in the early 1900s. When they finally figured out who I was and what line I was descended from, one of the men jumped up from the bench and exclaimed, "I know who you are! And, girl, don't you ever let anybody tell you that you aren't a part of this family." That seemed like such a strange thing to say, but now that I know my mother's story, I understand why he made that statement.

The story I had heard was that my grandfather, Joe, had been accused of raping a white woman in Louisiana and the KKK was after him. Joe Traylor escaped the KKK and had gone to Detroit, Michigan where there was family. He got work at the Ford Motor Company. The vigilantes eventually located him there and were inquiring around the company one day and word got back to Joe that some men were looking for him. He left immediately and began his trek west to California. He changed his name to Joseph Rowe and became a successful building contractor in Richmond and Oakland. To this day, many of the houses he built are still standing.

When Joseph Rowe had earned enough money, he sent for Agnes and her two children by another marriage. Together they began their life in Oakland. The first story I heard was that my mother was born to Agnes and Joseph Rowe when they lived in Richmond. However, I discovered a different story — my mother was really the offspring of Joseph and Rosa, and Joseph was my Grandma Rosa's cousin.

Rosa's mother, my great-grandmother, was determined that her daughter would have a good life and she would make sure that Rosa would not experience shame because of an experience that she could not have prevented. My great-grandmother was a strong and determined woman who protected her children at all costs.

When Rosa's parents drove across country from Detroit, Michigan to Richmond, California, they did so in a Model T Ford truck. The men in the family had constructed a wooden camper to fit on the truck bed so the family of seven could ride, sleep, and eat there. They called this vehicle, the Rowebus. This ingenuity and determination made it possible for Rosa to deliver her baby away from the scrutiny of the family's community in Detroit. Over the years, I heard about the Rowebus adventures from Rosa's brothers and sisters, but they never divulged the fact that they spent three or four months in California with Joe and Agnes Traylor so that Rosa could have her baby. This baby turned out to be my mother.

The Rowebus adventure of this African-American family trudging across roads of America, going west in the early 1900s, must have been something to behold. There was no sophisticated system of interstate highways or freeways back then. Black people were not able to rent hotel rooms or eat at restaurants in many cities and towns of the United States in those days. Even if they could have had access to hotel rooms and restaurants, this large family could not have afforded the cost. The

Rowebus was the mobile home for this family of seven, and it included one pregnant thirteen year old girl, my grandmother.

In my thirties I would occasionally visit this extended family of "cousins" and they would be unbelievably excited about seeing me. I never understood why there was such excitement to see me, especially since they really didn't know me. "Cousin" Lois took me in on those visits and was always anxious to oversee my stay to insure that it was as good as possible. "Cousin" Margaret also enjoyed having me come for a stay, but I never got to know her as well as I did Lois, probably because Rosa lived in a condominium complex across the hall from Margaret during the latter years of her life. "Cousin" Rosa was always pleasant but had little to say to me. Back then I did not question her reserve; I just thought that was her manner.

Grandma Rosa must have had many emotional and internal struggles whenever she saw me or my brother Alan. We were the only two, of the four children in my family, who spent any time with our people in Detroit. Grandma Rosa had been married for many years, and she and her husband lived in Chicago, Illinois. They adored each other and had a wonderful life together. They had no children of their own, and Rosa's husband never knew her secret.

It was many years before I discovered Rosa's secret. I had been visiting my favorite cousin in Detroit, and she took me to see her mother Jessie. When I met Jessie, I stood in front of her in shock. I said to her, "You look just like my mother!"

She simply nodded yes. Jessie was deaf, but she could read my lips. A guarded smile came over her face, and, at that moment I knew that something was not as I had been told regarding the Rowe family. After all, my grandfather's real last name had been Traylor; he had changed it for purposes of escaping the vigilantes who were searching for "Joe Traylor". Now, standing here before me was evidence that my mother and her children were actually also connected to the Rowe family. My mother looked just like them – just like Jessie.

That evening I sat on the edge of my favorite Detroit cousin's bed, and she against the pillows, as I tried to decipher the puzzle of what I had seen that day. The story I had been told suddenly did not make sense. My mother was the spitting image of my cousin's mother, "Cousin Jessie". My cousin allowed me to explore many hypothetical scenarios about what had happened, but she kept the family secret a secret.

When I returned home to Arizona, I called my mother to tell her what I had discovered and tried to find out the true connections. She did not deviate from what she had told me in the past. She only said that there had been quite a bit of inter-marriage among the Traylors and the Rowes, a possible explanation as to why she and Jessie looked so much alike. About a year before Rosa passed away, my favorite Detroit cousin told me the story that solved the mysterious secret about my mother. Rosa was in fact my grandmother *and* my mother's biological mother. The people that I thought were cousins immediately became aunts and uncles, and I now had so many cousins that I could identify closer to me in lineage! By the time I knew Rosa was my grandmother she had become senile, and my visits to see her were for my heart only. There was no real dialogue between us; yet, I was happy to be in her presence, even though we could not speak with one another.

When Grandma Rosa passed away, I went to her funeral with the understanding of who she was. Seeing her lying there in the casket was a very sad experience for me because we had never had the opportunity to know each other well. I am sure in my heart that we would have loved each other. What I do know is that she was a kind woman who worked to put her two younger sisters through college. She always gave of herself to everyone else, and she had a heart of gold. I am so glad that I know that she was my grandmother.

I now understand why my family held such a sad secret, and I have great admiration for all of the people involved. My only regret is that I did not get to know Rosa as my grandmother, and my biological family never really got to be part of our larger family. I remember my mother saying once that, if we had had an opportunity to live in Detroit with her large family, none of us would have gone through the trials and tribulations in our lives that we experienced in California. The family would have been supportive of my father and mother so they would never have felt the anguish and pain of being somewhat alone in their struggle. My paternal grandmother, grandfather, and Great Aunt Betty were in our lives and, of course, I loved them. Unfortunately, they were unable to provide the kind of a big family like the Rowes had in Detroit.

At Rosa's funeral, my cousin informed everyone that Rosa had a daughter, who was Thelma, my mother. People were shocked because most people did not know that Rosa had a child. A few people knew, but most did not. My cousin did not want her Aunt Rosa going to her grave without the truth being told. She also explained about the decision that had been made for Rosa's benefit because of the times and how taking her to California to have her baby meant that she was able to have an honorable life. The only person who spoke to me during the social gathering after the service, was Rosa's only surviving brother Robert. He told me that he was glad that I had come to his sister's funeral.

Understanding the family secret brought me a sense of peace, yet it did not diminish the connection that I have to Agnes' family members to whom I am not biologically connected. I still love them deeply. I always knew there was a secret in my mother's life; I just did not know what it was. I remember my mother telling me once, "Sarah, you think that telling the truth will make everything all right, but that's not true. Sometimes, even when you know the truth, there is nothing you can do about it. Knowing the truth does not always make things all right."

I remember wondering at the time, *What was that all about?* Her statement did not make sense and it seemed she was chastising me for telling the truth. Truth-telling was one of the values that I was born with, I think, and it was often criticized by my mother.

I understand how social mores and cultural customs of the early 1900s would have hurt a 13 year-old girl's ability to have a normal life if it had been discovered that she was pregnant. It would have also been hard on all the family members. The intervention of her family gave Rosa the opportunity to have an untarnished future.

As for my mother, she was raised by a loving mother in Agnes and a father who was a successful contractor until the Depression hit. My mother's parents had intended to send her to the University of California but, by the time she graduated from high school, her father's business had long-since been closed down and he had moved out-of-state. In an effort to remain financially afloat, my mother and Agnes ran a curtain laundry out of their home in Oakland.

In the 1920s and 1930s, people had lace curtains and shades at their windows. These curtains required washing and then stretching on a frame with pins all around to catch the curtains as they dried. These frames were called curtain stretchers and people had their curtains cleaned in this manner by curtain laundries.

The income from this curtain laundry did not generate enough money for my mother to go to the university. I think that not being able to go to the University of California was one of her biggest life disappointments. Her life would certainly have been much different had she had that experience. Today I have forgiven my mother for all the nasty ways she treated me and I carry only love in my heart for her. When she died, I realized that I had been grieving a relationship with her that I had wished for for a long time. I understand now how difficult her life was and that she had hopes and dreams for a better life. She kept many more secrets about her life, but we did not know about these secret traumas during her lifetime probably because they were too painful for her to talk about. Knowing about her pain helps me understand the possible reasons for her mean treatment and unkind words. My mother thought she was preparing me to live life as an African American woman in a white world. She believed this required a different kind of preparation than my brothers needed. Still, the constant rapids of our relationship were extremely tough for me.

I think the worst thing I experienced from my mother was when my father was dying. I had flown to Sacramento from the east coast to see my father after he'd had a severe stroke. I drove my mother across town to the hospital, and we sat in the car talking before going into the building to see him. She said to me, "I don't know why you think your father is so great or why you have forgiven him for the beatings. You weren't such a good little girl; you deserved everything you got."

I could not believe what I had heard, especially since I was about to see my father on his death bed. I turned to her angrily and said, "No child deserves what we got as children." I wished that I had said, *How dare you say this to me as he is lying in the hospital after having a stroke. What a terrible thing to say to me at this moment!* I was so emotional and stunned by her words that I could not speak what was really in my heart.

I live in Northern Arizona, now, and sometimes I must travel to the east coast for my work. The day before my mother died, five years after my father had passed away, I was in Baltimore on business. I had been working and knew that she was having a difficult time. When I called that afternoon to see how she was doing, her voice was very weak and she asked me to come to Sacramento right away. In that instant I knew that she was dying. I tried to get my brother to take her to the hospital but he refused. He also refused to be by her side, saying she wanted to be alone. Though I was very angry by his refusals, I wondered whether this was an agreement that the two of them had made; that she would be alone and not be taken to the hospital. It would be like my mother to do something like this. There is a part of me that respects a person's right to have that choice, but I just didn't know about it, that is, if there had been an agreement between them.

I arranged to have someone cover all of my appointments for the next few days and I took a flight to Sacramento. There was a layover in Phoenix. While I waited for the connecting flight to Sacramento, I called my mother. Her caretaker answered and was clearly upset. She told me that my mother had passed away during the night. I called my brother and told him that I was going home and that my husband and I would be there the next day. I asked him to please wait to plan a service for her and to dispose of her belongings until I arrived, when together we could make all of the arrangements.

When I arrived in Sacramento, I was aghast to find that he had, in two days, hurriedly emptied out her two-bedroom apartment. There was nothing left. He had given most things to the Goodwill. He had totally wiped the hard-drive of her computer clean so that the instructions she had written for after her death were not available to anyone but him. My mother had a file on her computer which was meant to tell my brother and I how she wanted her assets dispersed. She had given the name of the computer file to her caretaker, but my brother insisted that he was the only one who knew of my mother's wishes. My feelings at that moment were of disbelief that this was happening.

I remember that on one of my visits to Sacramento to see my mother, she said to me that she had "fixed everything" and that she was going to enjoy looking down on us to watch the fighting and bickering that was going to take place between my brother and me. When she said that, I did not know what she meant. When I walked into that empty apartment and, in the ensuing hours when I was trying to figure out what was happening and trying to put the pieces together in my head and heart about what was occurring between my brother and me, I remembered that moment. It was so hard to deal with, and I just couldn't believe what had happened.

Everything that occurred around my mother's death led me to think back on how difficult our relationship had been. This was not unlike many times before; the only difference was that my mother had now passed on. I have such regret that my relationships with family members had not been more positive. However, these relationships and the experiences of my life with these family members have helped me sort out the things that are really important and the things that are not. It has all been a test for me to truly learn forgiveness, compassion, and love, for these are the most important things in life.

Lessons Learned

Some people may be unhappy that I have exposed the difficulties of life with my family members, especially the discussion of the challenging relationships that I had with my parents. We have been taught in our culture that we should not publicly discuss the difficult parts of our relationships, especially regarding parents. I wrestled with whether to share my story but finally decided that I would not be able to authentically write about the why, what, how, or when of my personal development without explaining these relationships. It is the truth-telling to ourselves that I believe is so important and necessary to our personal growth and development.

My Story

I have learned over the years that it was important for me to tell myself the truth about what was happening in my life. I also needed to figure out my role in the story and how I had contributed to the outcome. In other words, what was my part? In the past, I usually looked outside of myself to try to figure out my truth. I admit that I had difficulty reconciling the truth about my relationship with my parents, and it was only after I confronted the truth about my reality and the growing that I needed to do, that I was finally able to begin making a healthy and whole plan for my life. It is important to acknowledge that we are each on our own journey. My parents had their own journey, as did my brothers, as do I.

I realize now that my experiences with my family happened so that I could learn important life lessons. The main things I have learned are: (1) I needed to develop self-esteem and learn to honor and trust myself; (2) I needed to set boundaries and not let people walk over me; (3) I needed to know that understanding and telling my truth is absolutely okay; (4) I needed to learn how to love, forgive, and trust myself; (5) I needed to believe and trust that God is with me at all times, and (6) I needed to learn that Light is *always* stronger than darkness. Eventually, I was able to stop blaming others for the difficult experiences in my life as well as taking the abuse personally. I am not saying that I am a Miss Goody Two-Shoes, but I did come to understand that if I continued to carry negative feelings inside, it would have a detrimental impact on me but not on anyone else. Wrestling with these emotions was about trying to survive. It was about trying to turn my life around. The most difficult challenge was to overcome my abusive childhood and, as a result I have finally learned to ignore most of the negative messages that come from others. I have learned to be discerning about those messages and to accept what was helpful and release what was not. This has not been an easy task, but I finally realized that, in order to live a better life, it all had to begin with me.

My difficult life experiences taught me that there is a God that I can trust. I couldn't see God or physically feel God, but I had begun to ask for things like open parking spaces and they showed up. I know this sounds trivial, but when you think that you might be all alone during difficult times in your life, even parking spaces seem significant.

It may sound strange, but I learned a great deal from the abuse I experienced as a child. As an adult, I have learned that I can walk into a new setting and read the environment almost immediately, and my perceptions are most always right. Almost instantly, I am able to determine who the players are. I have the gift of "reading" people by feeling their energy and having a good sense of who they are. I have learned in recent years that I not only receive my own messages, but I also receive messages for others, and I have learned to trust this gift. It mostly happens when I am talking to someone heart-to-heart.

My Story

I carried many feelings and coping behaviors from my childhood into adulthood. I had no sense of my self-worth or personal power. I gave away what little I had. I had little confidence or self-esteem. The only way I knew to behave was with great fear that was reflected in my need to have everyone like me and to do nothing that would be unpleasant to anyone. It was difficult to please everyone else all of the time. Much later in my life I finally realized how important it was to please myself.

It wasn't until I was in my late forties that I began to set boundaries with people. In the past, most people treated me like a pushover. That doesn't happen anymore. I have learned to tell the righteous truth, most often in a way that is kind. It is not my intent to hurt anyone in the process of truth-telling but, when necessary, I can be very direct and intentional about my expectations.

The experiences in my life gave me great empathy and acceptance of people. I understand the pain of others. I learned to read what is behind another person's action and to hear what is not being said. I am intuitive. These qualities came from having what were difficult life experiences, and I have come to understand the value that my difficult experiences brought to my life and I am grateful for them.

My second husband often teased me about my desire for and expectations of living a harmonious and peaceful life. Yes, I did want harmony. I believed that if I was not causing chaos or bringing drama into my house, then harmony and peace should prevail. I learned that my expectations were not always realistic, mainly because other people did not have the same goals. I could only have that expectation of myself. I could be a peaceful person and have personal harmony; I just could not expect that other people in my life had that same intention or that they would behave the way that I wanted them to.

I came to understand that peace and harmony had to reside within me, no matter what anybody else thought or how they behaved. I did not have to fight others in order to live a peaceful and harmonious life. Through prayer and meditation, I could be peaceful and harmonious inside. I began to recognize that it all started and ended with me. Today people tell me that they like being around me because I exude a calm presence.

My experiences could have been much, much worse. I endured what I needed to in order to learn life lessons and become the person that I am today. I have been told that we are always where we are supposed to be. For a long time, I could not, for the life of me, understand those words or that concept because, quite often, I did not want to have the experiences that made up my life. I had a lot to learn, and all these years later I get it.

When I was in my fifties, I received a photograph of myself as a baby. I don't have many pictures of myself, but this photo is precious to me because it shows me crawling forward on my grandmother's bed. I am looking back at someone, and there is a light above my head. I am sure the light is from the camera's flash; still, it is shining over my little head. I love this photo.

I have looked at that little baby photo often and have asked her, "What are you thinking?" and "Who are you?" When she decided to "speak" to me, the message I received was, *You came here knowing it all, and with an understanding of who you are, not what or who other people think you are. Know it, believe it, trust it, love it. Be all that God means for you to be in the world, always.*

It has taken me quite a while to be able to embrace this message. I needed to discern and reflect on the good, the bad, and the ugly experiences in order to sift through what I needed my life to be. From now on, with God's help, I am committed to making good choices. I don't always succeed, but my intention stands. When I don't achieve my goal, I try to cut myself some slack and move on to the next opportunity in life.

The truth of that message from the baby girl in that photo has set me free to be generous of spirit. I encourage you to allow that little person in you to speak so that you can fully be who God intends you to be in this lifetime. I believe that while we live in our body, we carry our soul's message. I believe that this message has existed for longer than we know. We have all been given much. Being still and quiet with baby pictures can help us access our soul's message. Allow your soul messages to be quietly revealed to you.

I know that no matter how difficult our life circumstances are there is always someone experiencing something far worse.

That reality does not minimize what we are going through, for everyone on the planet faces life challenges. These experiences will not crush us, if we can appreciate that there is a purpose behind each set of circumstances and that we can rise to make the best of difficult situations. Other people play important roles in our lives because we have things to learn from our experiences with them. Again, we are never alone as long as we trust God's powerful, all-knowing and loving presence. Faith is the key.

Today, I am grateful to God that I have been able to forgive those people in my life who were often mean and abusive toward me. I understand that they were doing their best. I carried pain, anger, fear, and disdain for their abuse for many years. I have now come out on top of those experiences and I carry only forgiveness and love in my heart.

To take this understanding to a higher level, let me say that I now appreciate that the experiences we have are actually greater than us. We need to move outside of ourselves to understand how we can apply the lessons that we have learned from these experiences in order to help others, or to make a difference in the world.

When I apply this thought beyond my own personal life, I truly understand how the experiences with my parents have helped my ability to be a career and life coach. I have a greater understanding of what others are going through because of what I have gone through. I have a greater ability to be empathetic, while at the same time challenging my clients' behavior to help them move forward. Because of my own experience, I know that it is important not to remain stuck in self-pity, for that gets us nowhere except deeper into self-pity. My goal as a career and life coach is to help people strengthen themselves for their own good. The trick is always to be able to move outside of ourselves, myself included, in order to consider how we will serve.

I think it is amazing that my parents were able to keep it together for as long as they did. There were definitely rough spots all along, and some of those experiences played themselves out in ways that two of my brothers did not survive. The brother closest to me in age eventually committed suicide and my youngest brother succumbed to his generation's fascination with psychedelic drugs which kept him from developing a stable lifestyle. Eventually he died from heart complications. Those years left indelible marks on all of us.

As I think about the years of my growing up, I am deeply grateful for my parents and the struggles they endured throughout their lifetime. Somehow they kept a roof over our heads and food on the table. I cannot imagine what it must have been like trying to raise a family of four children during those times. They had no support from family or friends, even to baby-sit, let alone anything else. Their peers were trying to keep their lives together too. I now understand what my mother meant when she said to me one day in her later years, "We didn't have the benefit of Dr. Phil on television."

Life Lessons From My Mother

When I was in high school in the late 1950s, many of the Caucasian girls in my class got summer jobs in downtown Sacramento at the department stores and I wanted to do the same thing. My mother apparently decided this was an opportunity to teach me about racial differences and inequities. I had not grown up in the South where I would have confronted issues of discrimination on a constant basis.

Mother took me downtown to put in applications for summer work in the department stores. As it happened, we only went to one store. She instructed me to go into the Kress department store and ask to fill out an application. When I did I was told that all of the jobs were filled and that there were no job openings. I went back outside and told my mother what the woman had said.

"Well, did you ask to be placed on a waiting list?" she asked. When I told her that I had not, she sternly instructed me to march right back into the store and tell the woman that I wanted to be placed on a waiting list for any job opening that came up. I was very scared as I went back inside. Immediately, my fear became tears of pain and sadness because I suddenly understood that I was being discriminated against.

Although somewhat subtle, discrimination against African American people was very real during that time in California. It was not the South, and there were no "white only" lunch counters, drinking fountains, or bathrooms. However, in many ways, there definitely was discrimination that was sometimes overt and sometimes subtle.

I can just imagine how my mother felt about making sure that I had that experience at Kress. After that episode, she arranged for me to get a job cleaning a house of one of her white co-worker's daughters for the summer. Today I have great admiration for all people who clean houses for a living. At that time, however, it did not feel very honorable, as my high school counselor had told me that there was no need for me to enroll in college preparatory classes because all I was ever going to do was grow up to clean houses anyway. Cleaning that house during the summer of my junior year of high school made me feel like I was living out the counselor's prophecy. I resented my mother for getting me the job and hated every Saturday morning during that summer when I went to work. Though I went with a smile on my face, I was not a happy camper. Today I know that that was a good experience for me. I am not above doing any work that is honorable.

Gratitude to John – Another Faith-filled Walk

My brother John committed suicide when he was thirty-five years old. After his death, I discovered, intuitively, that he had been gay, but I had not realized this during our growing up years together. As a family, we did not honor gay people, and John heard the demeaning remarks we made about them. When he was twenty-five years old, he "divorced" our family. He told us that he no longer had a family and that we were not to be in touch with him. I was greatly pained by this, and I cannot imagine what my parents must have felt. The only thing I could do was try to keep up with where John was and send yearly birthday and Christmas cards. He always responded by asking me to leave him alone.

After John's death, I asked my mother whether she had known he was gay; her answer confirmed my intuition. She said when the coroner came to tell them of his death, she and my father had to clean out his apartment. She found and read his journals that told of his relationships. Her response when I asked if she had known was, "Yes, but he didn't come here that way." I felt a rush of sadness for John, my mother, and for all of us.

I still feel sad that I did not love John fully when he was alive, for whom he was as a gay man. I have since wondered what we as a family would have done, felt and said had he told us. I have attempted to rectify my ignorance by asking God and John for forgiveness and by working for the rights of gay, lesbian, and transgendered people.

Today I do not listen to jokes or engage in conversation that would be demeaning to gay or lesbian people. Although I have not lived in their shoes, it is important to me that I understand their struggles and, as I am able, to advocate for their right to live with equality and the same rights as any heterosexual individual, for, in God's sight, we are all equal.

Another brother took drugs for many years during his life and died from heart complications. This was my youngest brother and he was the apple of our mother's eye. She called him her "sunshine." I have another brother who is still alive, but our relationship has suffered over the years. My siblings and I chose different paths with what we were given. Over the years, I have felt sad that we did not grow into adulthood with the close family relationship that I had wished for my whole life. What I have come to understand is that everyone does the best they can with what they have been given at any point in time, and, in actuality, we are all playing our roles impeccably well.

Paying attention to relationship dynamics and how we interact with each other can be a tremendous training ground. If we can be open to the possibilities, we will realize that our family experiences have given us countless opportunities that can help us to live our best life. It takes courage, to say the least, to use this information with personal honesty, integrity, and strength in order to receive the lessons that God is teaching us.

Mother Introduces Me to Advocacy

Three years after I graduated from high school, an ad hoc housing advocacy committee was formed in Sacramento to assess the level of housing discrimination in the downtown area. This was in the early 1960s when the State of California began to racially integrate many of the executive and managerial positions within state government service. State government employees who were in charge of integrating those managerial positions had not faced the fact that people of color, specifically African American people at that time, were having difficulty renting apartments and purchasing homes in the State Capitol.

My mother introduced me to the ad hoc group called State Employees for Equality. We went out in pairs, one Caucasian and one African American, to canvass neighborhoods, block-by-block. I went to apartment buildings on one side of the block while my Caucasian counterpart went to apartment buildings on the other side of the block.

Once we had visited each apartment building we compared notes. My partner had been shown and offered rental opportunities in all of the buildings that she canvassed, while I had been declined in all of the buildings that I went to. The State Employees for Equality submitted a statement to the State of California Department of Employment that then helped bring about changes in Sacramento so that all new employees who were people of color were better able to find adequate housing. This was my first active advocacy effort.

Overcoming Inferiority

After many years of experiencing emotional abuse I did not have a sense of self-worth, self-confidence, or an understanding of who I was. I always questioned myself and apologized for every little thing, even when I had done nothing to be guilty or ashamed of. I was afraid of my own shadow. My stomach was always tied up in knots. Somehow I knew that I absolutely had to overcome my fears and feelings of inferiority. I knew that I needed to work to change my behavior. I had to find a way to take control of my life. After much thought, I decided I needed to develop a script of words that I would use whenever someone tried to define what they thought I should do.

I thought about all of the people in my life who had tried to define my beliefs and actions. In the past, I would have taken what they told me and did whatever they said without question. Inside I would be seething with anger and resentment or feel insecure. From my perspective, I knew that I had to make another decision about how I would function in order to stand in my own personal convictions and personal power.

One day the message came to me about what to say in my script. It may sound simple, but coming up with the following response was huge for me. The simple script that I repeated to others was, "Thank you for your suggestion. I will give it some thought." Sometimes I would include, "I'll get back to you on it." My little script used to infuriate my mother because I was clearly saying, *I will no longer blindly accept your messages, because I am developing my own.* This polite and personal strategy worked and helped me become more confident. I was no longer trying to measure up to someone else's thoughts and opinions while struggling to find my own opinion or to make a decision.

This personal standing-up-for-myself process taught me that

I did not always have to have the answers, and that my answers did not always have to be right. I also learned that I could change my mind anytime I wanted to, no matter what anyone else said or thought about it. Believe me when I say that my new way of being was very hard for some of the people in my life. In the beginning of this new strategy, I sometimes struggled to remember what to say, and I would quake in my boots out of fear of what might happen. Still, this change was just what the doctor ordered and exactly what I needed to boost my self-confidence.

Now realize, I could definitely change my mind, and that I did, over the weeks or months and even years. My shift in attitude and thinking did not imply that I didn't know what I was talking about in the moment. Despite how others criticized me or tried to characterize my behavior, I did what was right for me; yet, it did not mean that I was flakey or undependable. It didn't even mean that I was not sensitive to their wishes, because I was. I simply changed my mind. The gift of this experience was that I made a conscious decision to grow and to risk changing my behavior.

This personal growth led to my ability to set relationship boundaries, which was a healthy thing to do with certain people in my life. I can accept that everyone may not like me for this, yet I am living in the approval that I have for myself according to my own deeply held values and personal integrity. I no longer betray myself because I have learned to stand strong in myself. I am now a person that I like very much, and I am grateful that God helped me get through the maze of my earlier life so that I could make a difference in the lives of others.

Work Experiences After High School

From the earliest time that I can remember, I wanted to be a teacher – an elementary school teacher. When I was in junior high school, a student teacher program was developed that made it possible for me to be a student teacher at the elementary school I had attended. I so enjoyed helping others to learn that I wanted to go to Sacramento State College to obtain my teaching credential. But life took interesting turns and teaching elementary school children would not be my path. Still I know that I am a teacher. I just don't teach in a traditional classroom.

My father was unemployed when I graduated from high school. One month after graduation I was fortunate to land my first job at the Sacramento County Hospital as a clerk typist in the medical transcription department. This job made it possible for me to help the family financially. My mother had insisted that I take typing classes in high school so that I would always be able to take care of myself. That was excellent advice.

I still had the dream of becoming an elementary school teacher, so, after a year of working at Sacramento County Hospital, I enrolled at Sacramento State College. I was a part-time student while remaining a full-time employee. My position as a medical transcriber was the first on-the-job training experience that would lead to a test in medical terminology. For two years my co-workers coached me and after four attempts, I finally passed the test. I felt so ashamed the first time I failed the test, but the saving grace was that my co-workers taught me the facts of life in business. They taught me to be tenacious and not ever give up a goal that I had set for myself. Passing the medical terminology examination would increase my salary and also give me a skill that was marketable. It was an experience that I have never forgotten.

Challenges at home and work left me with little time to devote to college, and the reality was that I just could not keep it all together. After three years, I eventually left college and decided that I would go back if I ever had the opportunity. I definitely needed to keep my job and do it well. At the time, I could be happy working as a medical transcriber for the rest of my working career. I enjoyed the challenge of the medical terminology and the knowledge that I gained about what I was typing and reading. My co-workers were wonderful and the Sacramento County Hospital was a good place to work. But I could not have imagined the life that would open for me; one right after the other, each position building for the next opportunity.

Life at IBM

After four years of working at the Sacramento County Hospital, I received a call from a friend who worked at the IBM Corporation in San Francisco. She told me that there was a secretarial position available and asked whether I would consider applying. I applied and was hired immediately. I moved to Berkeley because I was afraid to move to San Francisco, which seemed so big and so fast. The reality is that there was nothing in my life that had prepared me for living in San Francisco. I assuaged my own fear by saying that I wanted to live in Berkeley because there were trees and grass, the pace of life was more in keeping with what I thought I could handle and the cost of living was less.

My experience with IBM provided me with an incredible life opportunity. I was like a sponge, observing all of the people and everything going on around me at the office. I had never been exposed to people who skied every weekend during the winter, though invariably someone came to work on Monday morning wearing a cast. I worked with a woman who lived in the St. Francis Hotel. She was driven to and from work in a limousine every day. Back then women wore suits, gloves and hats to work. It was a totally different world than I had ever experienced. My mother's *at-home charm school* had really prepared me to fit into this work environment because at least I understood how to dress and interact with these people. It was necessary to be a very keen and observant "student" of the business as well as the social culture in the workplace.

As a medical transcriber, I had learned to type 120 words a minute. In this IBM environment there was no other secretary who had the typing speed and accuracy that I had. The other secretaries on my floor were not happy that I had been hired and they did nothing to introduce me to the universal filing system or other systems that IBM had throughout the entire company. These women did everything possible to sabotage my existence there. However, there were others outside of my specific office who embraced me. They taught me to play bridge during our lunch hours. And, in my attempt to be accepted, I began to smoke cigarettes. It was such a dumb thing to do because I had had asthma as a child. But I wanted to be accepted and become one of the gang. Thank God I was able to quit smoking years ago, even though it took several attempts.

Eventually I moved from that particular department and was made the building receptionist. I was very surprised to be placed in this high visibility position. It was a fun job and I got along well with everyone who came into the building. Also, I was such a fast typist that I could take on work that other secretaries in the building could not complete. I enjoyed this work for as long as it lasted.

After about a year, I was transferred to the Oakland IBM office, which was closer to home. I was promoted to secretary for a marketing manager and systems engineering manager and all of their staff, which numbered about forty to forty-five people. Somehow, I figured out the IBM processes and functions that secretaries needed to be aware of, no thanks to my colleagues. I don't know what happened. It just all seemed to mysteriously come together for me. I did such a good job in Oakland that I won an IBM Means Service award that had not been given to anyone in several years.

While I know that I did exceptional work, I think I won the award because I confronted my boss about the affair he was having with the clerk typist who sat next to me. I had to cover for her and do all of my work too as she gallivanted all over the building each day. Covering for her meant answering a "call-director" that had almost 100 incoming telephone lines for our office. These lines went to our branch manager, two marketing managers and two systems engineering managers and all of their staff. My neighbor's desk alone was a huge responsibility, and when I added that to my secretarial duties, the task was monumental.

With the onset of computers and all, it is staggering to think about what we did in the early 60s with equipment that is antiquated now. A "call-director" was a big box which was at least two feet wide by about one-and-a-half feet deep and it sat on the desk about three-quarters-of-a-foot high. It contained all of the back-up telephone lines for every person on the floor. When the phone was not answered by the intended person who normally received that call, it was answered by the "call-director" person. The phones rang constantly. The person responsible for answering "call-director" phone lines was like the operator for our floor. The woman who sat next to me obviously did not want to do her job.

During that time in my life I was not normally a very confrontational person. I prided myself on being nice and considerate to everyone, but I was angry about this situation and it seemed that no matter how many times I talked to my boss about it my office mate gallivanted more. I think she enjoyed showing me who had the upper hand.

Over several months my frustration grew so much so that I finally gathered the courage to talk to the branch manager as well as the four other managers in the office about my dilemma. They all said that they couldn't do anything about it. Finally, I had a conversation with my boss where I threatened to write a letter to the president of IBM in White Plains, New York if things did not change. IBM's president often sent the message across the company that he was always available to hear our complaints and that he would do his best to straighten them out. He did this because he did not want a union inside the company.

I received the IBM Means Service Award just before I planned to send the letter. Shortly before I was scheduled to receive my award, I was asked by two IBM men who were forming their own company to go to work for them. They were leaving IBM and they wanted me to be their first employee. It seemed to be a great opportunity that I could not pass up.

Working For a Start-up Company

Working for Computer Synergy, Inc., taught me how start-up businesses work. This experience has continued to be invaluable to every position that I have held since then, and it certainly helped me when I began to work as a consultant in later years. I worked for this company until they grew to seventy-five employees. In the early years, I was responsible for every administrative aspect of this company from human relations to accounting to interfacing with our customers.

At Computer Synergy, Inc., I learned that I am good at getting things started and having the vision to move the agenda for projects. I learned that I am a committed employee who will move heaven and earth to get the job done. My understanding of business principles, procedures, and products grew tremendously. I had excellent relationships with the customers. Much of the experience and expertise that I gained from this position has been applicable to many jobs in my work career and to the development of the consulting company that my husband and I eventually formed together.

Work Life in Arizona

In 1980 I moved to Phoenix, Arizona with my five year-old son and began work as a job developer for the United States Catholic Conference. My work was to place Southeast Asian refugees who were new to the United States into the job market. Working with people who had to flee their homes and their country was an incredible experience. Many of them had suffered the great loss of many family members to war. It made me very grateful for all that I had in my life. I worked through an interpreter most of the time and had a very successful placement program. My program was eventually taken over by the Arizona Department of Economic Security. Before my program was absorbed into the DES, I was recognized by the United Nations High Commissioner on Refugees for having one of the best job placement programs in the country. I was asked by different job placement programs in the U.S. to consult with them to help improve their programs.

Refugee people taught me so much. Even though many of them were depressed from the ravages of war and displacement from their homeland, they wanted to make their own way and figure out how to be successful in this new land. They were eager to please their employers and eager to make a new, successful life for themselves. Often they were able to translate skills they were experts in at home into the new world of work in the United States and I helped represent them to employers.

More often than not, I received the message from Arizona employers that they had no problem hiring Southeast Asian people that I was placing with them. Employers said that these people were more reliable to work with than their American counterparts. I found this quite disturbing and it made me realize that I needed to develop a program that could help *all* people prepare for the world of work, not only refugee people. That is when my coaching career began, though at the time it was called employment counseling.

I developed a new program through Lutheran Social Ministry called JOB MART. I have to admit that I was filled with fear to begin such a program. There were so many people who needed help preparing for the work world, as unemployment was very high during that time.

I had a friend who was a pastor in Phoenix who kept pushing me to develop the program. He tried to help me overcome my fear about mucking around in other people's lives. In actuality, I was afraid of failure. My friend finally said that he was going to put up $3,000 of his own money to help me out. That was a lot of money back then. He told me that he had a couple of volunteers for me. Another friend, who had been a teacher, wanted to work with me part-time to learn how to do the work. In other words, people in my life wanted to support me and make sure that I had no excuse to not create this program. Indeed, I had to put my fears behind me and develop the program to serve the employment needs of people seeking work. There were so many people who needed help. JOB MART turned out to be a very successful program. We helped hundreds of unemployed people.

One of the best tools I bought was an inexpensive full-length mirror. I put it up in my office so that people could see themselves as an employer would see them. My question to them was, "Would you hire *you*, if you were the employer?"

One incident stands out in my mind because it was so power-ful and confirmed for me that I was doing work that could make a difference in people's lives. My first client, a young woman in her mid-twenties, had just been discharged from military service. She was overweight, had long stringy hair, and generally did not present herself well. Her work background was good and she could be very saleable to prospective em-ployers because she had good skills, but, clearly she needed to groom herself better.

I remember confronting her in a very kind way about how she came across. I arranged for her to have a haircut and style from a beautician who donated her services to my clients. I referred her to a boutique where she could purchase very nice clothes at a discount for her interview. When she came back for her next appointment with me she was very excited. She looked beautiful. She went on to tell me that she also went to her first Alcoholics Anonymous meeting that week prior to her appointment with me. I was so excited because she recog-nized what she needed to do in order to change her life and to be successful in her job search.

I found that people really appreciated hearing the truth as I saw it. I often told clients that it was not my intention to hurt them but to help them be successful. Doing this work with hundreds of people was a real gift to me in that it helped me discover my passion.

In fact, the program continues today in Arizona under a new name called JOBNET. It functions a little differently from the program that I began, but it still helps people prepare for the work world and links them to potential employers.

My First Advocacy Work Experience

I thought I was going to work in the JOB MART program forever. It was such a passion for me. I loved counseling individuals about their work styles and ability so that they could more easily be hired in the workforce. However, after about four years of doing this work, a woman came to town to visit my husband Ed. He was the executive director of Lutheran Social Ministry of the Southwest, and she wanted to talk to him about starting a new program in Arizona that would provide a state-wide advocacy program for the Lutheran church. There were several other state offices in the country at that time and she wanted Arizona to join this network. Even though this woman came to talk to Ed, by the time she left our home, she had convinced me to become the first legislative advocate for the Lutheran church in Arizona. She and Ed were both ecstatic about my decision to accept this new position. In a certain sense, it was a pilot program to see if this work could be successful in Arizona.

I was so committed to being of service and, as I understood it, advocacy through the passage of public policy legislation, was one way that hundreds of people could be helped. I struggled with leaving the JOB MART program because I had such a passion for the work, but, I became convinced that advocacy work could also have a great impact on issues of poverty in our society and could possibly help even more people.

During this time, I often talked with my parents about my advocacy work and how surprised I was to be in this position. This was definitely a time when I understood that hearing about world events as a child at my family's dinner table contributed to my preparation for this position. I brought with me to the legislative advocacy position very strong commitments about helping to improve conditions for people who were living in poverty, though I did not really understand how the legislative process worked at that time. I had been told that what was needed for the position was a strong understanding of the poverty issues that people faced and that I could learn the legislative process while doing the job.

Needless to say, that was also one of the most frightening times of my work career. Though I had clear commitments about helping people, I was scared because I did not have this kind of work experience and had received no training in how to do the work. I had to make it up as I went along each and every day. In the beginning, I felt like an imposter.

One senator, in particular, laughed in my face, every time he saw me walking down the halls. After all, here I was a black woman working for the Lutheran church as a lobbyist. That was funny and out of place to him, a black person and Lutheran did not go together, from his perspective. The other thing that made this senator laugh is that there were no other religious advocates working at the state capitol, and *what did I think I was doing anyway?* However, he was very surprised when Father Ed Ryle came onto the scene from the Catholic Church about a year after I began my work as a religious advocate. It was then that legislators who had laughed at me began to rethink their treatment of me.

These legislators who made fun of me really had to swallow their teeth, though, when my husband and I were invited to a dinner where many of them were present. Although Ed, was the executive director of Lutheran Social Ministry, he was also a Lutheran pastor and he was invited to offer the prayer for this event. From that moment on they all treated me differently. It was so funny, yet so ridiculous and insulting, how that is what it took to have them back off and take me and my work seriously.

The entire time that I held the position of Lutheran church advocate in Arizona, I lived with tremendous fear. My initial thought about the job was not to focus so much on lobbying, but to do advocacy training in order to help Lutherans in Arizona understand that they could become advocates. The work I was doing needed support from Lutherans across the state in order to have any impact. At that time in Arizona's history, State legislators seemingly did not understand how to work with public policy advocates, especially those of the religious denominational stripe. It was important for me to communicate to them that I was there to help them gain support from constituents. Initially, I decided that I could accomplish more if I appeared at the State Capital each day.

When I wasn't at the state capitol, I was out in communities all over the state, training would-be advocates. With the help of the late Senator Jacque Steiner, we began a yearly program of Lutheran Day at the Legislature so that Arizona Lutherans could understand the impact they could have at the state level. State legislators began to understand that people really cared about what they were doing. Lutheran people began to understand that they could positively influence legislation that concerned public policy issues of hunger, housing, education, etc. It was a learning experience for all of us. Little did I know that this position was training me to work in Washington, D.C.

One day, our son Brad came home from junior high school and told me that he was afraid of black people. You cannot imagine my shock at hearing this from my son, who himself is black. When Ed came home from work I told him what Brad had said and we both agreed that it was time for us to move to a place where he could grow up knowing who he is as a black male person in America. Arizona, at that time, was definitely not the place. Ed and I decided that we would begin applying for new jobs in places that could help our son develop and grow into a whole, in-touch-with-himself, African-American man. As it turned out, we moved to the Washington, D.C. area. Ed became the President of Lutheran Social Services of the National Capitol Area, and I worked in the Lutheran Office of Governmental Affairs on Capitol Hill as an assistant director responsible for lobbying public policy issues.

Life Prepared Me for Advocacy Work

Listening to my parents talk about world events at the dinner table every evening, evidently planted the seeds of preparation to work as a public policy lobbyist in Arizona and then in the environment of government in Washington, D.C. Of course I had no idea that such work existed, much less how to prepare myself for this work, but it was the childhood experiences of those conversations that must have sunk into my curious mind.

I have worked in places that I never imagined possible. I have traveled around the world to some of the places that I recall my parents discussing, such as Ethiopia, Kenya, Malawi, the Caribbean, Hong Kong, Israel, Germany, Greece, Turkey, Italy, France, Switzerland, and the Philippines. I have been to most states in America. The memory of these experiences still astounds me. According to the rules of society and the normal preparation required to attain the experiences that I have had, I could never have expected to be in those or other places in my life. But Spirit has most definitely had other plans for me.

During my growing up years, my parents struggled every day to keep food on the table and a roof over our heads, and still, somehow, they were able to see the world in global terms. Mine was a very unconventional household for the time and place in the United States, and life experiences certainly prepared me for the work opportunities ahead.

Work in Washington, D.C. on Capitol Hill

Working in Washington, D.C. on Capitol Hill was one of the most incredible experiences of my life. During that time, I had the opportunity to be part of the lobbying processes that created the Family and Medical Leave Act and the Americans with Disabilities Act. We worked on Welfare Reform, though we were not totally pleased with the outcome. I was surprised that my responsibilities related to so many of the domestic policy issues that my family had faced, or people close to me had dealt with. I was part of a group of advocates that discussed ideas about the development of what AARP would become — whether it would be a membership organization and what services members could expect to receive.

Health Care Policy Reform during the Clinton Administration meant that I had to attend weekly meetings at White House office buildings. During that time, my colleagues in other religious denominational offices elected me as the national chairperson of the Inter-religious Health Care Access Campaign.

We worked very hard together as well as inside our individual denominations to inform and gain support for health care reform.

Once I was in a meeting with other lobbyists on health care reform in the White House Cabinet Room where I was seated directly across from President Clinton and next to Vice President Gore. This was a most amazing experience for me. I could not get past the personal issue in my head that said, *here I am, a black woman from Del Paso Heights, California who has not completed college, who did not have adequate access to health care as a child, and I am in a meeting sitting across from the President of the United States, trying to persuade him to support health care reform for the people of this country.*

In my childhood world I rarely saw a doctor simply because we could not afford one. When any of us got sick, my mother used remedies that she had learned of from "the old folks" to heal us. Economically, our family could have qualified for welfare, except for the fact that my father was living with us.

I was so unsettled by the whole experience; the reality of being in the White House getting ready to meet the President of the United States in the Cabinet Room, and the instant reflection of my life in Del Paso Heights all converged for me in an instant. It was overwhelming. In fact, a funny story that I will tell on myself is that I went to the meeting in the White House with a small camera so that I could have photographs of that experience. I was so excited when I arrived. The person leading our contingent scowled at me and then looked down at my camera. If looks could kill, I would have been dead meat. I immediately took my seat and tried to hide the camera under my chair.

In retrospect, it was pretty funny. For a moment I forgot that we had gone to the White House to work – to try to convince the President of the United States that we were there to encourage him to support our position on health care reform. Truth be told, at that moment, my only real contribution to the meeting was that I was the only person of color sitting at the huge conference table.

Health care reform was not passed during the Clinton administration. We had all worked hard with our respective organizations to gain support for our position. Along with other denominations and faith group organizations, we tried to gain enough support to make a difference in Congress. Sadly, we were unsuccessful.

The White House Cabinet Room meeting was an incredible experience for me. It was a watershed moment, as I was personally confronted with the realization of where I had come from and all that I had done in my life as well as where I was at that moment. I was sitting in the big leather chair of the Attorney General of the United States that had her name, Janet Reno, engraved on the back of it. It was absolutely mind-boggling to me that the Universe had moved me into such a position. It was an incredible time to be in Washington, D.C. on

Capitol Hill, and I could never have engineered this reality on my own, even if I had tried.

The message for me was to stay open and do my best because I had absolutely no idea where the Universe was going to take me next. My goal was to just keep putting one foot in front of the other and do my best to be receptive to how God was calling me. That also meant that I should do good work, make good choices as opportunities came my way, and remain focused on the lens through which I sought to be an instrument for God in the world.

I did not intentionally seek to be a lobbyist for any cause, and it still amazes me that I was led to this work. The only explanation that I have for being called to these experiences is that I had been educated by life in what it means to live in poverty - issues around the lack of food, health care, housing, etc. I can only think that God led me to these places as part of a greater plan of which I am not fully aware. My job is to simply follow the path before me and to say *yes* even when I am nervous and unsure of the opportunities I am being given.

We have all been given a unique set of gifts; it is up to us to use them as fully as we are able. I have set as a personal intention to use my gifts in service of others and in service to God at all times. This personal intention acts as the filter through which I discern whether I am following my path responsibly.

Being Unconventional

The most unconventional part of my life began when I married for the second time. My spouse is a Caucasian man, and we have been together for thirty-one years. Ed and I chose to spend our lives together because we love each other and are committed to the same values of justice and walk the same political path. But thirty years ago our decision was not popular.

You see Ed, is now a retired Lutheran pastor. When we married there was probably not even a handful of bi-racial clergy couples in the Lutheran Church nationwide, and we knew only one other couple in which the woman was black and the man was white. Ed and I were strengthened by the experiences that we faced over the years, and we always worked for what we believed.

We each know who we are, individually and ethnically, and neither of us tries to be something we are not. We have been extremely fortunate that our children have been wonderful about our marriage and that we all have truly loving relationships. We have a good time when we get together, like any other family. We just come in different hues; Ed's two adult children and my adult son, our in-laws, and grandchildren blend together to make a beautiful bi-racial family. It has not always been a bed of roses, of course, but we are who we are and it is pretty special.

I can certainly attest to the differences between white America and black America. My first husband of ten years was an African-American man who was an economist in California. The challenges that we faced were very different than my life of being a black woman living with a white man in America. My current husband has access to the American life in ways that my first husband never did. He could go as high up in the organizations he worked for without anyone feeling threatened by him because of his skin color, which is not the case for most African-American men in this country. He can travel anywhere he wishes without regard to how he will be accepted racially, though as a bi-racial couple we have been very careful in our travel in the South. Even so, our circumstance of being a white man married to a black woman has not been as threatening to white environments. White privilege definitely exists in America, and I have seen it through Ed up close and personal. I am grateful to Ed, because he is sensitized to this reality and, for the most part, understands how he has access to the benefits of living in America in ways that people of color in America do not.

I am proud to be an African-American woman; yet, I perceive the world differently than many of my friends of all races and cultures because of the experiences I have had. I see myself as a global citizen and have come to understand that all people on the planet are doing the best they can. This does not mean that they cannot do better; it simply means that they are doing the best they can right now. Hopefully, we will all be able to do better, for we all want the same things for ourselves and our offspring no matter what culture or environment we live in.

When Ed and I were first married, he was invited by the Jewish Federation of Greater Phoenix to visit Israel on a study tour, and I got to go along. It was the first time that either of us had traveled outside of the United States.

Growing up in Del Paso Heights, California, I had not known any Jewish people. I grew up thinking, *They're white; so what's the problem? You can't tell they are Jewish from looking at them. They just look white to me.* This was my naïve opinion until traveling to Israel.

Here is the story of my journey to the Holy Land. It was Jewish government policy that anyone visiting the Knesset must first go to Yad Vashem: The Holocaust Martyrs and Heroes Remembrance Authority. I was thirty-six years old, and it was the first time I had personally been confronted by the fact that there are people in the world, other than black people, who have also been brutalized, oppressed, and killed for their ethnicity. I learned, then, that oppression and brutalization is found all over the world.

Being in Israel for two weeks and walking through Yad Vashem was truly powerful. Everywhere I went, everything I saw and experienced about Israel, I saw through the lens of Yad Vashem. I feel that I am a changed person for having visited Israel.

The experience of Yad Vashem opened me to be the best life and career coach that I can possibly be with all people, whoever they are. It has become increasingly important to me that we all understand our personal power and that we are present in every life situation because each and every one of us hope for a good life no matter what our experiences have been in the past.

I have traveled to refugee camps throughout the world and have seen the worst of what people of all races and cultures do to each other. I believe people must gain the courage to do better and to live peacefully with our sisters and brothers. I live my life knowing that I choose to see each person for the loving being that they truly are.

Wrapping It All Up

As life presented itself I had a number of jobs that eventually put me on a career course that I could never have imagined. Reflecting back, I have the distinct sense that God has been steering my course all along so that I would have experiences that would build one upon the other. While I did not earn a college degree, I have earned many degrees in *life* that have prepared me to assist others on their path. I continue to be grateful beyond measure for all the opportunities that present themselves.

When my husband retired after fifty years from the Evangelical Lutheran Church in America, I left Capitol Hill and we began work as consultants in The Naylor Group. We have been doing our consulting work in various ways for the past thirteen years, because we both believe that we must continue to be of service until we are no longer able to do so.

Life continues to be an incredible adventure. In The Naylor Group, I have worked as a consultant for five years for AIDS National Interfaith Network. I worked on an assessment team with other consultants to help the Robert Wood Johnson Foundation determine how effective their Interfaith Volunteer Networks have been across the country, and I have worked for the past ten years as a consultant for the Federal Office of Personnel Management on leadership assessment teams for senior managers and executives in federal service. All during this time I have continued to provide life and career coaching for private clients. I am so grateful for each of these experiences. Throughout the years and during all of the work, Ed and I have lived in Silver Spring, Maryland, Shepherdstown, West Virginia, and most recently in the Sedona area of Arizona. Our children are all adults and we have three grandchildren. We live happily with our little Shih-tzu dog, Sam.

Being of Service

Everyone on the planet faces life challenges, for that is what it means to be alive and human. No matter what we are going through, there are others who are facing their own challenges. There is no need to make comparisons. These difficult experiences will not break us, as long as we can know that there is a purpose behind them and that we can rise up to make the best of it. We are never alone, providing we trust the powerful, all-knowing and loving presence of our Source. It is with this kind of faith that I can love those people who have been difficult for me to understand.

I have finally gained confidence in my abilities and I love who I have become. I am a generous and forgiving person and no longer fear living my life to the fullest. I have forgiven my parents and other people who have been abusive toward me in my lifetime and I no longer hold on to any of those experiences because today I know and understand in my heart that God has walked with me through my life with love, guidance and protection. It is clear to me that I have crossed the rough waters of my life so that I may have the joy of helping others. I am grateful to be of service.

BE-ATITUDES
Attitudes for BEing

As the concept of this book was manifesting, I was intuitively *given* a series of *BE* intentions to include in the writing. The guidance was profound and exact and had powerful implications for a life well lived. It occurred to me that these *BE* messages were reflections from the other side of the river. These messages are about how we are to *BE* in our lives rather than what we are to do. Though many of us are aware of the biblical verses that refer to the Beatitudes, these messages relate to *Attitudes for Being* our best so that we can live our lives successfully in the eyes of God and in our own hearts. *Crossing Rough Waters* and making it to the other side with a straight back is possible when we carry love in our hearts. It is this love that provides the bridge to the other side of the river.

BE Faithful

When I talked about how this book came to be, I mentioned the conversation I had with Jo. She asked me if I was going to write the book that I had been told to write. Over the years and before meeting Jo, I had been encouraged to write this book by a few different people. Each person asked the question of me without knowing that I had been asked before, and none of the people knew each other. Now, the question came to me again from Jo. The only difference this time was that Jo put her question and statement to me into the context of crossing the rough waters of life. She said, "When you have crossed over to the other side of the river and your back is still straight, you have the obligation and responsibility to God to tell others how you made it through."

For the first time, I understood that I had a responsibility to write this book – for the greater good. Jo's message helped me take this writing task more seriously. In my personal examination of what I was being asked to write, I realized that my entire story was about faith, my faith in God.

As I have thought about Jo's question, I have come to the following conclusion: I don't believe that having a "back that is still straight" means that faith is measured physically. I believe that having a "straight back" refers to the faith, trust, courage, and fortitude that is required to get through the rough patches in life with a personal constitution that remains mostly intact.

Crossing the rivers in life requires vigilance and inner strength. It requires a belief that you will come through adversity and that there is something outside of yourself that you cannot see or touch that is going to help you get to the other side of the river by helping you find the bridge you need to cross.

In order to get to the "other side of the river with a back that is still straight," I believe that we need a belief and faith in something that will provide the hopefulness and personal resolve needed to help us get through the chaos and turmoil in life, because sometimes the pressures in life are so great that we need help from an unseen higher power. In my life, I have called this higher power, "God." Others might call this force by another name. Some people think they can do it by themselves, but, when we are in the deepest despair, and there seems to be no one or nothing else that can sustain us, that is when a higher force outside of ourselves can help us get to the other side of the river.

It has been important to me to have faith that this source exists. In the darkest moments, when I didn't think I would survive this journey, I just had to trust that God would help me make it through. There will be times in life when the only thing that we can do is turn the challenges of life over to this higher power, for we are not in control. Indeed, I have come to understand that I cannot control anything or anyone and it is my faith in God that has helped me cross the river and arrive on the other side with a back that is still straight.

A magnificent force created all that exists. If there is any question about this, look closely at the beauty of a single flower. Consider that your body breathes in air and needs water in order to exist. It is that basic and impressively complicated at the same time.

Humanity struggles to understand what it means to respect and honor itself, but I believe that if enough of us can come to live in a way that honors a belief in something bigger than ourselves, then our faith and prayers can change the human condition and together we can become more than we ever imagined.

We can become:

> A world of people who honor each other;
>
> a world of people who respect Mother Earth;
>
> a world of people who live without borders and welcome the stranger;
>
> a world of people who share the earth;
>
> a world of people without judgment;
>
> a world of people in which everyone has food, water, shelter, and good health.

A Deeper Understanding of Faithfulness

In a conversation with a close friend about the concept of faith, she said, "You know that biblical verse that says, *To whom much is given, much is expected?* We discussed and pondered over this verse in relation to our lives. During our discussion, we realized that we both had always thought the verse meant that if you were given much of the world's riches and had an idyllic life, full of love and security, you were required to "give back" to society.

We came away from our conversation with a totally different understanding and interpretation that applied to each of us. That evening we clearly understood that "because our backs are still straight," it is our responsibility to give back by helping others understand how to come out of extremely difficult life situations and become a whole, stable, and a fun-loving person.

My friend and I understood that the pain we experienced in

our own lives was not about something we created intentionally; we were just trying to survive it all. Upon reflection, there seemed to be a divine plan in our lives because we were given many experiences and much information through those experiences so that we could tell others about the level of faith that is required to make it through the biggest challenges of our lives.

I believe that, with God's help, all of us can make it to the other side of the river with backs that are still straight. With faith, much prayer and love in our hearts, we can cross our rough waters of life and get to the other side of the river.

BE Unique

We are all unique. This means we have no equal among us; there is no one in this world that is exactly like another person. We each possess unique gifts to share. Think about it. What is your special uniqueness? What are your gifts?

Knowing and understanding our uniqueness shows us that we do not always fit into a particular mold or group. We are not supposed to fit in. It took me a very long time to understand this. When I was younger I always tried to fit in with this group or that group, because I did not have the courage to be different. Today I understand that I am different. I think it is actually fun to affirm the uniqueness of another person and to affirm my own uniqueness. Differences are what make the world go round. If we all enjoyed doing the same thing or being the same way, can you imagine how boring our lives would be?

Today, when I have a job to get done that requires a team effort, I intentionally look for people whose strengths are different from mine so that together we have the best opportunity to fully address whatever task is at hand. Living in community and working in teams can provide the strongest opportunities to experience wholeness when we are able to recognize unique differences among us and then capitalize on those differences.

When we find ourselves in a loving group with the same people, we are very often reluctant to disrupt it in any way. The group has developed a unique quality about it and we are reluctant to disturb that formation, because each person has brought his or her own unique qualities to the group and there seems to be a real fit. When we find this fit, it is so exciting. I think we are able to fully enjoy and benefit from this experience when we also recognize the special qualities that we have and how we can best contribute to this group.

In order to live fully in who we are, means that sometimes we must have the courage to risk being different, unconventional, and authentic. Follow what seems best for you. We must be who we are by being true to ourselves. Take time to honestly assess all that you are, and see what is most important to your life path. Take the time to honor your unique self.

It is important that you *hold your own council* about how you feel about yourself. Loving and honoring our uniqueness helps us walk comfortably in our own skin with confidence. Show the best of who you are, for you are a valuable and resourceful person. Own and *Be* your unique self.

BE Awake

Being awake to Spirit is a very tall order. Living intentionally in that awakened state is an even taller order. The personal goal to live life from this perspective requires a certain personal intention and consciousness. It is akin to having a personal guidance system that points us in a positive direction at all times, especially if we recognize its pointing power. Living in an awakened state means that we try over and over again to live outside of our ego self. We must resolve to live from the place of Spirit within us. This is a tricky proposition. It requires a great deal from us, a particular mindfulness.

Awakening is challenging. We can sometimes feel the blocks of fear and protection that we have erected in order to keep ourselves safe. Fear-based living keeps us constrained and constricted. Fear does not allow us to tap into the best part of ourselves. At some point, if we are honest, we need to love ourselves enough to feel that wonderful person hiding deep within behind the fear.

When we allow ourselves to embrace that part of our self that we have not acknowledged and let out, then we can begin to see greater possibilities for our life. Loving ourselves enough to emerge from our cocoon can bring forth a most surprising life. We just need to make good choices and allow the best to happen. Love yourself. Awaken.

Being awake does not require that we have all of the answers. Thank Goodness! It does not require that we always have to be right. Being awake to Spirit's guidance says that we live our lives so that we understand that every event provides an opportunity for us to learn. The important thing is to live life in such a way that we ask the question, *What is this situation trying to teach me?* Very often in my life it has turned out that the more challenging the situation the greater the lesson I had to learn. I did not come to understand this immediately. The biggest lessons I had to learn were revealed to me years later.

Being awake to God's presence assumes that practically every person that we come in contact with either has a message for us, or that we have a message for them. Over the years, I have learned that God speaks to us through our relationships, through our encounters, and oftentimes through the environment of the natural world of plants, animals, water, rocks, and the mountains.

One of the most challenging things is to have the eyes to really see what is before us and to have ears to hear even the slightest message? Receiving these messages is not easy. It takes a lot of practice to become sensitive to awakening to messages that are oftentimes unspoken. By that I mean being sensitive to unexpected events that are occurring in our life. Oftentimes I have found that there was no way that I could have begun to engineer a particular outcome. All I could do was be amazed by how things worked out.

When I began to understand that I needed to pay attention to new people that I came in contact with, because they either had a message for me or I had a message for them, my daily walk became much more exciting. Every time I flew on an airplane, I paid attention to who my seat mate was. Invariably, I would get off the plane taking my new best friend to meet my husband. He was never as excited as I was.

Here is a little story of being awake to what I might learn: I had traveled to Baltimore from the Southwest to work as a leadership coach. It turned out that I had a free day before beginning my work, so I decided to call Jackie, a friend whom I had not seen for over ten years. We decided to have lunch in Washington, D.C.'s Union Station, one of my favorite spots in this city. Jackie and I had worked together for seven years when I was on Capital Hill for the Evangelical Lutheran Church in America as a lobbyist for public policy issues. We had much to catch up on.

One of my primary goals of this visit was to hear how she and her extended family felt about the inauguration of President Barack Obama. I was trying to feel vicariously what it was like to live in D.C. again, especially with this awesome new historic development. So, I left my hotel in Linthicum, Maryland and headed for the MARC train station near the Baltimore-Washington airport. I had only taken the train to D.C. one other time from the Baltimore line, so I did not feel sure of myself. There happened to be a young woman standing near me who seemed very approachable, so I asked her if she was riding the train to Union Station. When she said that she was, I asked if I could just follow her so that I would get on the right train.

It turned out that I rode with this young woman all the way to Union Station. On the way, she shared with me that she had gone to college in Washington, D.C. and loved it, but she was now back home in Tennessee to complete her goal of getting a degree. She had returned home because she could no longer afford to pay the out-of-state tuition. We talked about her plans and I wanted to leave her with encouraging words because she was still making decisions about what she would focus on for her studies. Her primary goal was to be of service in the world. I told her that I thought such a goal was a wonderful intention and that the destination is important, but she should also enjoy the process required to reach her goal. And then I remembered a favorite line in a movie, "The Great Debaters," when one of the students was told, *you do what you gotta do until you can do what you want to do.* My new friend loved that line and wrote it down.

This young woman left me with words of wisdom as well. She and I had been talking about the difference between achieving perfection and working for excellence. She agreed with me that it is very hard to ever achieve perfection in anything, but, her comment to me was that hard work and intention can help us progress toward achieving excellence.

I was so grateful for this particular conversation that day on the way into Washington, D.C., but it wasn't until I was actually engaged in my work process with the coachees that I realized why and what that experience had been for me. My new friend had given me the exact message that I needed to share with each person that I would work with in the coming days. I have used this concept that she gave me in many coaching sessions since that time.

It turned out that each person I worked with during the next few days felt that they were not doing the best that they could do. Each of them said, "There is always room for improvement" and "we can never achieve perfection." Consequently, none of them were able to give themselves the highest achievement rating on the instrument we were using. I spoke with each person about the concept my new friend had shared with me: It is important to strive for excellence.

My process of learning how to live an awakened life has involved personal journaling, meditation and prayer. Other people attend classes that they find helpful. I often suggest to people that they try writing at least five affirmations each day, and repeat them every day until they can add to the list.

The process of awakening requires vigilance. Sometimes we make it, and sometimes we don't. Your journey is unique and each experience you have will not look or feel like another person's experience. That is why it is so important for each of us to embrace that which comes to us in our own way. I think that awakening to God's Spirit is a life-long journey. It is not something that one ever completes. I believe it requires courage to live an awakened life.

BE Transparent

Being transparent means being willing to see ourselves truthfully and to behave in such a way that we are guided by that truth. If we are truly transparent, then it is not comfortable to put on a mask or a show that doesn't honestly represent who we truly are. If we are being transparent, then it isn't necessary to be what we think someone else wants us to be. When we are transparent we allow others to really see our heart and soul. Of course the world around us will sometimes influence us, but we can still let our heart lead us. Being authentically who we are is the name of the game.

We Give Others What We Love

Because we give others what we love
nothing is wasted. Between us a rhythm –
the wingbeat of an eagle,
our hearts surging skyward.
And though we come timid
among stars in the different shapes of God,
of ourselves we offer everything
for the pleasure of this rising
for the pleasure of loving.

Carla Riedel

BE Confident

Having personal confidence means believing in yourself while possessing an element of humility. I lived too many years of my life without confidence because I compared myself to other people. When I did this, I could not measure up to what I saw in other people. I also came to realize that I had not identified the gifts that I had been given; instead I was identifying the gifts, skills and abilities that other people had and then I tried to live what I saw other people doing. Needless to say, this didn't work for me.

My lack of confidence was a big problem that I knew I had to overcome. I read everything that I could find in the self-help section of bookstores about confidence. Then I practiced what I learned over and over again until I felt confident. This process took several years before I began to ever feel somewhat confident.

The biggest thing that helped me overcome my lack of confidence was when I made the decision that I would approach new situations believing that I could accomplish them. I visualized myself being successful. I was very careful to give myself positive self-talk and silent encouragement about things that I had previously not done well. I began to do things that I had shied away from in the past. I agreed to take on responsibility for projects that I would never have done before. I never rejected an opportunity to take on work because I realized that I had so much to learn about processes and approaches that I did not know or understand.

All of this became a huge learning experience for me. I had to learn how to effectively communicate via public speaking and in writing. This was challenging, to say the least, but I asked for help when I did not know or understand what I was supposed to do. The more I chose to practice what I needed to learn, the more confident I became.

I realized that confidence doesn't mean that we have to master everything, but it does mean that we can do good work and do it well. It doesn't matter what our parents thought, or what our teachers told us about ourselves. It doesn't matter how we were made to feel earlier in our lives. What matters is that we give ourselves permission to strive for excellence and confidence.

Somewhere I read that the trick to gaining confidence is to make a plan to do the project that we have been afraid of or unsure about and stick to it. Move through the fear, no matter how uncomfortable it may seem at the moment. As we move through this task and accomplish our goals and intention, we find that our self-esteem and confidence become greater. When the task is finished, we can feel good about the accomplishment. This gives us courage to go on to the next thing, and then the next. When we stretch ourselves enough, we gain muscles that we never knew we had and this gives us the confidence we need to move along through our life to the next adventure.

Confidence is yours. Yes, it is. Walk with confidence. Talk with confidence. Be confident!!!

BE Bold

Each one of us needs to know and trust that we have been given all the gifts we need, whether learned or innate, to be our best. Going deep within ourselves allows us to summon the strength we need to move forward. Loving ourselves for all that we know and for all of our life experiences enables us to be prepared for what we are facing at any given moment. Know that we are not alone in this endeavor because God walks with us. With that power we can proceed successfully to an incredible end result.

If we doubt our abilities to move forward then that doubt denies the intention that God had for our life when we were created. This is something that I really had to think about. This concept took me back to thinking again about how I am unique and to again identify my gifts, skills and abilities. Understanding these things about myself helped me move forward with determination to do my best.

It is important to dig deep within and be honest about what we find. Don't pay attention to the negative messages that we have received from others. Negative self-talk is not helpful either.

Celebrate yourself from your heart, mind, and body. Live boldly — walk softly.

BE God's Voice in the World

Be God's eyes, hands, feet, voice and whole body, in the world. Be God's intention for the best that we can be to serve in the world. I believe that we are God's instruments of peace; we are love in all that we do and all that we speak. I believe that it is important for each of us to strive to make a difference in the world and in each other's lives. Life is sacred and we can help each other cross the turbulent rivers of life in order to get to the other side of the river with backs that are still straight.

The Story of the Little Wooden Bowl

For ten years I served on the Board of Directors of Lutheran Immigration and Refugee Service. We traveled to refugee camps all around the world. I observed and was confronted by the worst situations – the horrible things that people do to each other; the necessities of life that are lacking in the lives of many people around the globe, such as safe drinking water, food, shelter, etc.

On a trip to East Africa I visited refugee camps in Malawi, Ethiopia and Kenya. During the time we were in Ethiopia, our small group flew from Addis Ababa to a little village where we spent the night in a "motel" before moving on to the camp. Since I was the only female in the group, the men decided that I should have the room with a "bathroom"; of course, because of the primitive conditions, this was just a hole in the floor. At night, from this hole in the floor came the largest, most indestructible cockroaches I have ever seen in my life. Needless to say, I slept with all of my clothes on and with the light blazing all night long. There were also gunshots from rebels outside throughout the night, so the cockroaches were the least of the disturbing foes.

The next morning, after a breakfast of stale moldy bread and coffee, we rode by caravan in United Nations vehicles to the Gigiga refugee camp. We were protected by men with machine guns riding in other vehicles in front and behind our vehicle during the entire three to four hour-long trip.

There were rumors that we were not safe because we rode in UN vehicles. Evidently, there were Ethiopians from the hill country who were very angry that Somalian people had crossed the borders into their country and were using their valuable resources of food and water. Consequently, there were many attempts made to destroy trucks bringing in much needed water and food. Refugee camp observers like us from the United States were not welcome.

Upon arriving at the camp I was immediately surrounded by hundreds of children as far as I could see. My Caucasian male compatriots stood watching in amazement, and even I was stunned by the frenetic energy all around me. The children were so excited to see me. I had not been prepared for this experience and, at first, I was frightened at first by the multitude of shouting children surrounding me.

After a few minutes a hush fell over the group as a stately, elegant, elderly Somali woman parted the crowd as she made her way toward me. She appeared angry. She shoved a little wooden bowl in front of my face, placed her fingers into the bowl, picked up pinto beans and let them drop one by one into the bowl. The sound of those beans reverberated in my ears.

I was so confused by the confrontation of the whole experience that I did not understand what she was "saying" to me at first. This woman reached into the bowl again and let the beans drop one at a time again and this time I understood. The message was: We have no food! We have no water! We have no homes! We are dying! We need your help and what are you going to do about it?"

My compatriots and I walked around the camp after that experience and saw the magnitude of the situation. I felt sad and helpless as I looked at people who were sick and did not have enough food or medicine. I was struck with the realization that they were dying. And, as if this wasn't enough, leaving the refugee camp on our way back to Addis Ababa, I was totally shocked by the crowd of people who had each packed belongings in small bags or tattered luggage so that they might be the "lucky" one that we could take back on the tiny plane with us. We had just one seat left.

It broke my heart to be on the plane, knowing that I could leave and return to a better life. Seeing all of the people crowded around our plane hoping to be the one selected to ride with us brought tears to my eyes. It turned out that a woman with an infant child was selected because the baby needed emergency medical care to keep it alive. We left that field where there was no runway to go on to the next place where refugee people were experiencing the ravages of war and struggling for survival.

I felt totally helpless in these experiences and many others that I have had in refugee camps around the world. But today I realize that I am not helpless. I realize that it is important to share the stories of refugee people all around the world, because I am reminded *there but for the grace of God, go I.*

I shall always remember the power of the little wooden bowl that touched my heart. I shared this story because it is one example of being *God's Voice in the World.* Mainly, though, it is one story about learning to be sensitive to how I can be used to make a difference in the world. Each of us is God's voice in the world, wherever we are. I believe that we are supposed to help those around us to have a better life, however we are called.

BE Loving

When we live a life of loving-kindness toward ourselves and others, we express the love of God in the world. To me living with loving-kindness means that I live with the intention to carry love in my heart each and every day. I believe that we gain the most from loving ourselves and that the greatest gift that we can give is to love others.

Before my mother lost hope for a better life she once told me, "Sarah, there is something to love in every person that you meet in life. Take a moment to find what that is and then compliment it. As you get to know that person better, there will be more things that you can find to love. No one is perfect, so it is important to hold these loving thoughts about each person so that you are able to continue to find and see the best in them. Always feel loving thoughts for them in your heart." My mother's words have stayed with me and continue to guide me in how I try to meet and interact with people who come into my life. I have come to understand that everyone lives a life that has some level of challenge in it. I think it is important to ask ourselves what it would mean to walk in their shoes. Their life challenge helps me feel compassion and love in my heart and this activates my thoughts about how I can be helpful to ease their situation.

I believe that if we could allow ourselves to know another person's story, we could develop and live with greater compassion for each other. If we only knew another person's story, it would bring us closer together rather than tear us apart. Being willing to take the first step to share some aspect of our life story is often all that is needed in order to bridge chasms of misunderstanding or distance between people. That which keeps us apart can also bring us together in love.

Sharing Our Stories

I have a friend whose name is Lloyd. We met when I lived in West Virginia and became the best of friends. Lloyd was referred to me by our mutual friend Gary because my husband and I needed some work done on our farmhouse and Lloyd is an excellent handyman. When Lloyd came to our door Ed answered it and told him what we needed to have done.

To hear Lloyd's account of that experience, "...and then you came to the door, and I thought, what has Gary gotten me into this time?" He was surprised by the fact that Ed is white and I am black. Lloyd grew up as a poor white person in West Virginia who hated black people. He hated black people because when he was a child he had to get on the school bus at the last stop, and, by the time it reached him, it was full and there were no more seats in the white section of the bus. He always had to find a seat in the black section of the bus where he got beat up every day by the black kids.

Lloyd's daughter married a black man from the Caribbean Islands. When he and I met, Lloyd had not spoken to his daughter for many years, nor had he gotten to know her husband or his grandchildren. He missed the early years of his grandchildrens' lives.

144

Something told Lloyd that he was supposed to work for us that day when he knocked on our door. He and I began talking to each other in that first meeting on our front porch. We talked and talked for several hours. He had to come back the next day to actually do the work because we had spent so much time talking. By the end of that first day, we had shared so many stories and touched each other's hearts in such a powerful way that it was clear we had created a special bond. Lloyd loves his daughter deeply and I told him that it would be a shame to lose this relationship forever because of his prejudiced attitude about her choice to marry this black man from the Caribbean Islands. We talked about how much he was missing in his life by not acknowledging his grandchildren. From that moment on, Lloyd decided to call his daughter and ask for her forgiveness. He has done the work to develop a relationship with his son-in-law and grandchildren. They now spend time together and Lloyd enjoys playing with his grandchildren. He told me that he goes to his grandchildren's school and "dares anyone to say anything about *his* children."

Lloyd and I have a very unlikely friendship. He is a white West Virginian. He is very smart but talks like the stereotype of a West Virginia man with little formal education, and as a result of this, people tend to underestimate him. He is one of the smartest, most compassionate and loving men I know.

Lloyd has planted a garden so that he can share food with people in need. He sets his price for handyman jobs based on what he sizes up a person's heart to be. If he finds out that they have lots of money and a closed heart, he charges accordingly. He loves animals and respects their power and their heart. When you meet Lloyd, you also meet Spanky, his little dachshund doggie who is always by his side. I have seen him turn down jobs if someone didn't like Spanky or vice-versa. Lloyd is a wonderful man and he is one of my best friends.

The message I am trying to get across is that, because Lloyd and I risked sharing our stories with each other, we were able to form one of the deepest and loving friendships that each of us has ever had in our lives. We risked being vulnerable with each other from the start. That vulnerability paid huge dividends. Over the years, Lloyd and I have developed a close sister/brother friendship. This friendship bridges race, intellect, economics, gender, life experience, etc. There is nothing that we would not do for each other simply because we dared to love.

BE Strong

People sometimes confuse aggression for strength. I find that oftentimes strength is reflected in one's ability to be confident, to be a quiet strength, to see the best in others, to make it possible for another person to experience their best. Being strong requires a sense of our own personal power and knowing who we are. Acknowledge the strength that you carry. Identify all of your personal and professional gifts and talents. Being strongly committed to the best in ourselves will produce many dividends.

All over the planet people are being challenged these days. Many people are struggling because of unemployment, health concerns, relationship issues, lack of food, lack of housing, and the list could go on. This is a time when people are being called upon to be stronger than ever before because change is happening in profound ways everywhere we turn. It is a time when we are being given an understanding of what it means to persevere so that we can overcome whatever adversity we face in our lives. Standing in our faith gives us the strength to be a positive force for good.

As we respond to society's issues, gaining a sense of our personal power can be very helpful. Getting in touch with our personal power so that we can step into it effectively requires personal truthfulness about who we really are. Personal power is about understanding God's gifts that were bestowed upon us to be used in the world. Personal power can help us become strong in our convictions, strong in our actions, and strong in our faith. With God's help, we can grow stronger in our commitments and convictions to be a better person. Having the courage to stand in our own strength provides us with a sense of hope and encourages others to live in the strength of who they are.

BE Open to Change

Change is a part of life; there is no avoiding it. Being willing to live with change requires courage. Oftentimes events in our lives bring on such tremendous change that we may feel fear, resentment and a sense of insecurity. If we lose our job, or if a loved one becomes seriously ill or passes away, or if the relationship that we have been in for some time begins to crumble, we can experience the pain, anger, or fear that this profound change brings into our lives.

How we handle change and the choices we make through change can either make us or break us. Faith helps us understand that we are not in control and that we are not alone as we go through life transitions. The changes we experience in life can be our best teachers, if we are willing and open to the possibilities that lie within those changes. Ask yourself, *What is the lesson here? What am I supposed to do for the highest good?*

Depending upon the situation of change, we can recognize the fear that we hold, move through it, and replace that fear with love; love for ourselves, love of God, love for the package that this particular change comes in, and love for the possibilities that can come from this change. This is an optimistic approach to difficult circumstances. Of course, we are not always able to immediately approach life changes in this way, but, when we can move through change in this way, it is a true blessing and we can be grateful.

When I was young I thought that when I got older, I would

have this or that figured out and my life would calm down. Well – not so. The older I have become, the more wisdom I have acquired by living through the changes that occurred earlier in my life. I have learned that living in the process and flow of life and not trying to determine all of the components of the destination can make life easier.

Do your best and give yourself grace, loving kindness, patience, self-compassion, and time to figure it out. When you don't know what to do next, do nothing. Pray or meditate on it. Allow space for God's answer to come to you – and it will. Just wait and allow it to come. There have been instances in my life where it took years for answers to come to me about how I could possibly rectify particular issues. As I was learning and living through the challenging times of my life, answers did eventually reveal themselves to me.

The greatest wisdom I think I have gained over the years is not to be afraid of the changes that occur in my life, for change moves in and around us and reminds us that we are indeed God's gift in the world.

BE Still

Be still and know that I am God. Most of us have heard this, but how do we apply it to our life?

I have always tried to get things done, but I don't always know what to do or which way to go in order to accomplish the goal. I have pushed the river against all odds. However, it seems that no matter how hard I pushed, nothing seemed to happen, certainly not my hoped for outcome.

A few years ago, someone said to me, "If it isn't working do nothing. Be still. Allow whatever is going on to occur in your life. The occurrence may provide you with an experience that you need to have. It may provide you with an opportunity to learn a very important life lesson. Just wait. Be patient. Know that you do not have all of the answers all of the time, and it is not possible to control everything in your life."

These days I have come to believe that there really is nothing I have control over. The key word is "control." I realize that we can make choices to move in this direction or that, but ultimately, there is a greater controlling force than we could ever imagine.

Sometimes it is helpful to consult with others who might have more experience about a particular issue but, in the final analysis, the decision to proceed belongs to each of us.

Another important thing to consider is that in our culture, much emphasis is placed on DO-ing rather than BE-ing. Often we think that we are not accomplishing our goals if we are not doing much. We fill all of our time with doing, doing, doing. Allowing ourselves to just be is something that our culture doesn't often encourage. I assure you that if you can BE, more than you DO, it will have a profound impact on your life, physically, emotionally, and spiritually.

An interpretation on Peace of Mind, taken from the Bhagavad-Gita says, *For those who wish to climb the mountain of spiritual awareness, the path is selfless work. For those who have attained the summit of union with the Lord, the path is stillness and peace.*

With this understanding about the way life flows, the outcomes in our life can be much better. Living as fully as possible, without being attached to outcomes, is a wonderful way to live our lives. It is fine to set intentions, but understand that there will probably be many twists and turns along the way. Accept the guidance that is possible from God. Trust those intuitive messages that come. Allow space for the power of Spirit. All is in good order. Remember to *be still and know that I am God.*

BE Present

Be present in this very moment, for the present is all there is. This very moment did not exist yesterday, nor is it present in tomorrow. I like to say that it is important for me to set intentions rather than goals, because intention means that I am putting my energy into achieving a particular goal. But setting this intention does not mean that achievement of the goal is guaranteed. When I set an intention, it means that I am hopeful, positive, and optimistic about reaching the goal.

Being present in the moment, and giving up control of what is to happen, encourages us to pray, to ask God and all of the angelic beings to be with us and help us achieve the desired outcome. Being present is a very active approach to living our lives, especially in our most difficult moments.

BE Resilient

Resiliency is the ability to bounce back from the ups and downs in our life. It is an energy we have in reserve to face times of crisis and stress. If we have too much stress on a continual basis, our resiliency reserve becomes depleted and this can lead to depression or burnout. It is very important to make sure that our reserves do not become totally depleted. Our resiliency reserve needs constant fortification so that we are able to face those challenges that come before us each day. If we feel fatigue, depressed, or burnout much of the time, this is a red flag that our internal resiliency reserve meter is more than half-way depleted. If we are experiencing any of these feelings, internal alarm bells are sounding off to let us know that it is time to change this condition. We have the power to increase our level of resilience.

One of the best ways to replenish our resiliency supply is to make certain that we are enjoying aspects of our life each and every day. This is especially true if we are feeling the warning signs. It is time to get moving and do those things that we find exciting. Reminders can help us get in touch with how we are feeling. Make signs and put them on your walls as reminders that you need more *JOY* and *FUN* in your life.

Sometimes I hear people say that they have to wait to have fun or to enjoy doing the things that they like to do because they don't have enough time in the day. They say that by the time they take care of personal, family, and work responsibilities, there is just no time left.

All of us can find one or two things that we enjoy doing each day, even if it is for just a moment. We don't have to read an entire book, we can read one or two pages. I am a person who enjoys sewing and needlework. I make certain that I am always working on a project so that when it is completed I have a great sense of accomplishment and completion. Do whatever you need to do that brings you a moment or two of joy and fun every day.

Keeping a list of things that you want to do for fun is a very good way to make sure that you have a reference point. When you have a moment or two, take a look at your list and do something just for fun. Be spontaneous. The point of having fun is that you create balance in your life. Fun is not just for children. Adults can have fun too. Enjoyment and fun work very well alongside the responsibilities that we have.

When stressful moments or set-backs appear in our life, we can avoid letting them take us down to rock bottom by reflecting on those moments of enjoyment that we have recently experienced. We can also go to our fun list and know that we can replace the feelings of stress with excitement and fun. Adversity provides the personal laboratory for our growth and development of our character. We can bounce back, for we are resilient.

I remember when I was a child, one of the greatest lessons that my father taught me was this: "Sarah, don't be afraid to make yourself vulnerable. Being vulnerable means that there is something that we do not know and something that we need to learn. It is the big person who is not afraid to admit that they don't know something. It is the big person who does not have to know all of the answers. Don't ever be a know-it-all." That lesson has stood me in good stead all of my life. And, later in our lives together, my father followed his own advice and apologized to all of his children for his earlier behavior toward us.

Do not be afraid to admit that you are learning. Resolve not to remain in the land of setbacks. Move forward. It feels good when we overcome a challenge. This is resiliency.

BE Forgiving

Forgiveness is huge and can bring miraculous end results. Forgive yourself and then, in your heart or verbally, forgive everyone that you have ever held anger toward or that you have hurt in any way. It is not worth it to carry anger around simply because in the long run you become the big loser. Carrying anger and pain can make us bitter people, so it is important for us to hold the intention to live with love in our hearts.

Sometimes forgiving someone can be the most difficult thing to do, especially when we have been so deeply hurt by them. In my life I have found that the people who hurt me the most were also people who had great disappointments or hurts in their own lives.

One of the most turbulent rivers that I have ever had to cross was when I forgave my parents for the way they treated me. It wasn't until I was able to get past the personal nature of their actions and to think about their lives and what their life experiences had been, that it became much easier for me to forgive them. When I could reflect on what their hopes and dreams had been and how they had suffered such disappointment in their lives, it was easier to release my pain and hurt because I realized that their behavior really had nothing to do with me. Their behavior had everything to do with their pain and life disappointments. I must say it again – it really had nothing to do with me. I did not mistreat them. But my brothers and I were the ones that they took their disappointments out on. It took such a long time to work through this process to arrive in a place of forgiveness. I am so grateful that I understand this now.

When I know that I have hurt someone else, I have gone to them and asked for their forgiveness. It is important to me that I not intentionally hurt anyone. In the past, when I held onto grudges or painful experiences, I was the one who suffered not the other person.

Personal truth-telling is the answer. One of the most difficult things that we must do if we are to cross the rough waters of life and make it to the other side is to be able to tell ourselves the truth about whatever is going on in our lives. Until I could tell myself the truth about what had happened in my life related to my family of origin, I could not fully understand myself and what my life path was to be. In addition to telling myself the truth about family members, I had to look at myself honestly. I began to acknowledge the truth about who I am rather than the messages that came to me from my family. I know today that we all played our roles in my family of origin impeccably well. If I had not had the challenging experiences of that life, I would not be able to understand, without judgment, the myriad ways in which other people experience their challenging lives.

I know that telling myself the truth has helped me heal. Telling myself the truth has helped me forgive. Telling myself the truth has helped me love more fully. The truth is that I never expected to have the truth revealed to me in the way that it has come over the years. Each time that something of significance happened, good or bad, somehow I knew to ask the question, *is this something that I need to pay attention to and is there something that I am supposed to learn from this?* Because of the revelations of these experiences I have grown beyond measure, and it is all good, even the most difficult realities. These things came to me for a reason. There is nothing that happens in life without a reason attached to it. I am able to get on with my life in a way that I would have never expected.

It is time to forgive everyone that we have ever felt anger toward, or held pain and fear over. Our inability to forgive another person means that we hold on to the anger and pain in our own bodies. I have learned the hard way that anger and pain I have held onto has affected my physiology. Through this whole process of holding on and then eventually being able to release pain and anger, I have learned just how profoundly my psychology became my biology. Doctors are very important and it is important to pay attention to their diagnoses. But, we can also understand that our bodies are speaking to us all of the time, and we need to pay attention to the messages from our body.

If we pay attention to our body, we can learn a lot about negative feelings and emotions that we are holding on to or have held onto from the past. There are books that are available to help us interpret old thought patterns that have led to dis-ease in our bodies. The book that has helped me the most in understanding these issues is *You Can Heal Your Life, by Louise Hay*. Understanding these thought patterns can lead us to a deeper understanding about forgiving ourselves and those around us. Forgiveness is one of the primary keys to healing our lives. Forgiveness is also one of the greatest things that we can do in order to bring love more fully into our heart and it allows us to express love more fully to another person. Be forgiving.

BE Accepting

By accepting other people as they are instead of trying to change them to match what makes us comfortable we are respecting who they are, and in doing this, we are offering them unconditional love. Accepting another person means that they can be who they really are and we will not judge them for this, whatever their philosophies or behaviors happen to be. We are only responsible for our own behaviors, philosophies, values, and attitudes; we can only change ourselves.

Accepting and respecting ourselves means that we have the right to be who we are. We can remove ourselves from any situation that is not respectful of us. Accepting and respecting ourselves means that we must set boundaries for ourselves so that we are able to maintain our equilibrium and grounding. It is so important to please ourselves first, and then we have more energy and resources to offer others. This is not selfish. It doesn't mean that we won't consider another person. It just means that we are respecting, approving and accepting ourselves. It means that we are placing importance on our own needs and trying to meet them. Then we can care for others around us.

In our society we are not often taught the importance of self-care and self-love. When we care for ourselves first, we then have more to give to another person. Setting boundaries and limits on what we will do and what we are not able to do at any given time keeps us in a mode of self-acceptance and self-respect. We cannot expect others to respect us more than we respect and accept ourselves.

Another issue in the subject of acceptance is not to have expectations of another person. In the past, every time I had an expectation for someone else's behavior, I was always disappointed. In actuality, it wasn't fair to the other person, nor was it fair to me. I had no right to set an expectation for someone else.

Accepting others does not mean that we have to subject ourselves to abusive and cruel relationships. I think that when we are accepting and respectful of ourselves, we will not put ourselves in situations that are cruel or abusive. It is perfectly fine to draw the line and remove ourselves from situations in which we are not being respected and treated well.

We are all doing our best with what we have been given at any moment in time. That is not to say that we cannot do better. But, at this very moment, we are doing our best. If we could, we would do better.

As we grow and learn our great lessons in life, if we are open to change and learning, we do better. If we are able to release any fear that we are carrying, we are able to do better. But, it is very important to accept the fact that we are all doing our best in this moment. When we fully believe this, we are then able to live with grace and compassion for ourselves and others around us. Not one of us is perfect. When we learn to accept this fact about ourselves and others, we then cut ourselves some slack and we cut others slack. This is not to say that we should not do our personal work in order to be better individually.

When we are able to live in a more self-accepting way, we are able to see the best in another person and tell them what we see that is positive about them. When we are more accepting, we are able to see the heart of another person and embrace them for who they are. We no longer live in judgment.

Can you imagine what this world would be like if we were more inclusive in our thinking? We would no longer judge and exclude people of different races or economic conditions, and we would not set up institutions that exclude people.

Can you imagine how you would have felt if your mother or father had been fully accepting of you?

Can you imagine what your mother or father's life would have been like if they had received full love and acceptance from their parents?

Can you imagine what kind of world we would live in if all the inhabitants of the world received acceptance for who they are instead of judgment? This is what we all wish for in life, to live our lives and receive the acceptance and love from those around us.

Imagine what your life could be like if you could accept yourself for the gift that you are that God created. Imagine. Be Accepting.

BE Sincere

Sincerity is a virtue that most of us strive for. When we are sincere we are honest and stand in utmost integrity. I believe that sincerity reflects the inner feelings of a person. Sincerity begins on the inside and then is reflected on the outside through interactions with others in our deeds and in the words we speak.

I think I came here to be a very sincere and honest person, for it is innately who I am. But in my home I was often criticized for being honest; admittedly, I was sometimes brutally honest, whether they wanted to know or not. I had to learn to be tactfully honest.

These days I tell my truth to people in ways that is not meant to be hurtful. If there is a possibility that my words might offend someone, I make sure that I preface the conversation with words that let them know that it is my intention to be helpful and then I share what I am thinking. I believe that sincere communication has to be sensitive to all of the parties involved in the exchange. My being sincere also means that I care about the other person.

One of the most turbulent rivers that I have had to cross was when I needed to figure out why I was sometimes betrayed by parents, brothers, co-workers, and some friends. Because I never meant to be hurtful, insensitive, or threatening in any way, I did not know what I had done to bring these experiences into my life.

In some aspect of my past relationships, I think that perhaps my truth-telling, in some of the interactions, was more than the other person wanted to know. I was not always sensitive to this. Other times it seemed that my interactions with people sometimes elicited responses that indicated that I had threatened the other person in some way. It was never my intention to bring discomfort of any kind into these relationships. I never thought that this would happen if one sincerely expressed love, compassion, sensitivity, or concern.

Sometimes we have expectations for how we think people "should" interact with us. But, *should* expectations are often met with disappointing or hurtful responses. I have also learned that it is not possible for everyone to like us, and vice versa. In earlier years I thought that I could win everyone over. Today I understand how unrealistic that is. These days I believe that we should say what we mean and mean what we say so that we communicate with as much integrity and honesty as possible; that way we communicate a deep level of sincerity. Being sincere reflects a sign of respect and truthfulness and it increases one's intention to provide the best in our self.

BE Peace

Peace is a state of calm, serenity, contentment, harmony, and an inner feeling of well-being. Peace can relate to a peaceful environment. I thought of this often as I traveled through the world's refugee camps and was confronted by the lack of peacefulness. But I am of the mind that, in order to achieve world peace or peace in any environment, peace must begin with the individual — *Let there be peace on earth and let it begin with me.*

Life is sometimes chaotic and requires great intention to not allow ourselves to be pulled into the chaos of the world. It requires determination and intention to move beyond the chaos. It requires recognition and acknowledgement of the drama that is in our lives that is swirling around us. When we can recognize it, it is then possible to resolve not to be caught up in it. We can choose to live in a place of peace, which is grounded and centered, yet not airy-fairy.

One of the greatest lessons that we can learn in life is to love ourselves, with humility, so that we can be at peace. We can continue to learn this lesson through having difficult times with other people. We have all been hurt by the behavior of others' words they spoke to us, or the ugly things that they have done. We eventually come to understand that these words and deeds don't make us who we are. They are not a reflection of us, unless we choose to take it on. Don't pay great attention to ugly criticism or behaviors. If we can do this, the negativity of life no longer has power over us. The funny thing in my life these days is that the ugliness from others rarely comes to me anymore. If it did, I wouldn't pay attention anyway. It makes me smile to write these words, because I understand now that we attract from others who we are. This learning has taken a long time to achieve, and I feel very good about it.

It is important for us to be open to learning ways that we can live in peace and harmony with everything in life. Because we are each different, this way of living will be different for each person. I am hopeful though, that living peacefully can be a very strong intention for each of us, in whatever way that works for us.

We can learn to be peaceful and live in harmony with all that is. This can be our life practice on a daily basis; to live in harmony and a new consciousness with and for our highest good. I say practice because I know that, for as long as I live, I will always strive to *BE PEACE* in the face of all that happens in life. This is truly a daily practice and something to strive for. Love ourselves and love others, so that we can be at peace. Live a life that is *PEACE*. Every step we take, every word we speak, everything that we do. BE PEACE.

BE Grateful

Live in gratitude for everyone and everything in our lives.

Every moment is special and can be magical.

It is all up to each of us.

Living with gratitude in our heart

can change attitudes about even the worst experience.

Living with gratitude is an important act of love.

The simple act of gratitude for even the smallest

things in our life

shifts us into being grateful for everything.

As we walk through our home look for the smallest

thing to be grateful for.

Reflect on relationships with friends and family and

consider how we are grateful for them in our life,

even if some aspects of these relationships are challenging.

Consider our life experiences, even the difficult ones and

ask ourselves what have we learned,

what experiences have we had,

how are we blessed and how have we grown?

Recognize things that bring us joy and be grateful for them.

IN CONCLUSION

I believe that we are alive, living each and every moment with gratitude, in order to learn our greatest lessons; how to love everyone and everything on earth, including our earth. Coming to this conclusion helps each of us work our way through many challenging experiences.

There is purpose in everything, even the most difficult things. Senator Ted Kennedy said, "The purpose in life is about living life on purpose." This is faith, and faith is what leads us through the rough waters of life to the other side. Perspectives, circumstances and attitudes can and will change. Have faith to understand that we can be brought through to a brighter tomorrow; know that there is a purpose and lesson in everything. Just ask God and then be willing to wait for the answer. Be patient. Faith and prayer are the name of the game.

Some Things I Know Today that I Did Not Know Before:

• I KNOW that the Light is ALWAYS stronger and shines brighter than darkness.

• I KNOW that our life walk is sacred and that we are constantly being given information. We just need to have ears to hear and eyes to see, figuratively and actually.

• I KNOW that we receive intuitive messages from the unseen world, just as we receive messages in what we can see, feel and touch. Others may not have the message that we are supposed to receive, though they can sometimes help us interpret our messages. In the final analysis, we receive our own messages. Sometimes we call this experience intuition.

• I KNOW that positive thinking is more beneficial than negativity. Believing that the glass is more full than empty makes a huge difference in the results we receive in life.

• I KNOW that personal truth telling will set you free to be the most incredible person and lead the best life that you can ever imagine possible.

• I KNOW that if we substitute fear with LOVE, it will make a huge difference in our lives. Every time you have fearful thoughts, just think about how love could make a difference and then carry those loving thoughts with you.

• I KNOW that we sometimes learn more from our life experience in retrospect than while we are going through the turmoil.

• I KNOW that optimism, faith, and prayer will get us through.

It has been my intention to write a book that offers perspectives on living your spiritual journey; moving from being a victim to embracing your life as a sacred experience. I think that it helps to consider how our beliefs inform our daily life. Living our life from this spiritual place is very important. I have discovered that spiritual living is a round the clock practice each and every moment of our days.

Living our life from this perspective honors that we are human be-ings, not human do-ings. This perspective acknowledges that we are living a life that is dynamic all of the time. From a spiritual perspective, God is giving us lessons to learn all the time. When we can step back from these lessons and the events they create to think symbolically about what this whole thing called life is ultimately about, we are then led to a much deeper understanding of what it means to be faithful. When we can do this over and over again each day, we are able to see the path for our life journey and the lessons for our life. I have discovered the hard way that, until we come to a place of acknowledging and learning the important lessons that are placed before us, we will be given the same lessons over and over again in different forms until we get it. We must see all of the good that we are, hold the good thoughts that we think, and then affirm ourselves by carrying love in our heart.

God's richest blessings to each of you as you courageously cross the rough waters of pain and fear to experiencing the freedom that comes from becoming victorious along your sacred life journey.

Be reminded. You are God's gift to the world. You have been created for this special work as you walk upon the earth. You are to be who you are, your unique self. It is the reason you are here at this moment. Whatever your life situation is, you must gather the courage to move past your fears. Be the person you want to see in the world. Live in love and the light of God. Stop trying to be accepted by everyone. Be the unique person that you are and then be in service with that gift, because your time is NOW!"

Deep Peace,
Sarah Payne Naylor

BOOKS THAT HAVE INSPIRED ME

AMMONDSON, Pamela
> *Clarity Quest: How to Take a Sabbatical Without Taking More Than a Week Off*. Simon & Schuster, 1999

BATESON, Mary Catherine
> *Composing A Life*. Penguin Group, 1989

BORCHARD, David C.
> – *Will the Real You Please Stand Up? Find Passion in your Life and Work*. Sterling House Publisher, Inc., 2006
> – *The Joy of Retirement: Finding Happiness, Freedom, and the Life You've Always Wanted*. Amacom, 2008

BORYSENKO, Joan
> *The Soul's Compass: What is Spiritual Guidance?* Hay House Inc., 2007

BROOKE MEDICINE EAGLE
> *Buffalo Woman Comes Singing*. Ballantine Books, 1991

CAMERON, Julia
> *The Artist's Way: A Course in Discovering and Recovering Your Creative Self*. G. P. Putnam's Sons, 1992

CHOPRA, Deepak
> – *Perfect Health: The Complete Mind/Body Guide*. Harmony Books, a division of Crown Publishing, 1991
> – *Unconditional Life: Discovering the Power to Fulfill Your Dreams*. Bantam, 1992
> – *Creating Affluence: Wealth Consciousness in the Field of All Possibilities*. Co-published by Amber-Allen Publishing and New World Library, 1993
> – *The Seven Spiritual Laws of Success: A Practical Guide to the Fulfillment of Your Dreams*. Amber-Allen Publishing & New World Library, 1994
> – *The Path to Love: Spiritual Strategies for Healing*. Three Rivers Press, 1997

DYER, Wayne
– *The Power of Intention.* Hay House, *2004*
– *Inspiration: Your Ultimate Calling.* Hay House, 2006
– *Change Your Thoughts, Change Your Life.*
Hay House, 2007

ELY, Karen
– *Daring to Dream: Reflections on the Year I Found Myself.*
A Woman's Way, 2006
– *A Retreat of My Own: Personal Retreat Guide.*
A Woman's Way, 2008

FISHEL, Ruth
The Journey Within: A Spiritual Path to Recovery.
Health Communications, Inc., 1987

GRADY, Harvey and Julie
Explore With Monitor: Lessons for Freeing Yourself.
iUniverse, 2008

GUNDERSON, Gary
Deeply Woven Roots. Fortress Press, Minneapolis
and Augsburg Fortress Press, 1997

HAHN, THICH NHAT.
– *Being Peace.* Parallax Press, 1987
– *Peace Is Every Step: The Path of Mindfulness in Everyday Life.* Bantam Books, 1991
– *Anger: Wisdom for Cooling the Flames.* The Berkeley
Publishing Group – Penguin Putnam, 2001
– *Journey Together: The Art of Building a Harmonious Community.* Parallax Press, 2003

HAY, Louise L.
You Can Heal Your Life. Hay House, Inc., 1999

LINCOLN, Kenneth and SLAGEL, Allogan
The Good Red Road. Harper & Row, 1987

LORD, Andrea
> *All My Relations.* Reprinted with permission from
> *News from Indian Country,*
> www.IndianCountryNews.com,1991

MARTINEZ, Carla; SOUSA, John; WYNN, Toni
> *Color Voices Place.* Mille Grazie Press and SeaMoon
> Press, 1997

McGRAW, Phillip C.
> *Self Matters.* Simon & Schuster Source, 2001

MYSS, Caroline
> – *Anatomy of the Spirit: The Seven Stages of Power and
> Healing.* Crown Publishers, Inc., 1996
> – *Sacred Contracts: Awakening Your Divine Potential.*
> Crown Publishing Group, 2001

ORIAH MOUNTAIN DREAMER
> *The Invitation.* Harper San Francisco, 1999

PEARSON, Carol
> *The Hero Within: Six Archetypes We Live By.* Harper &
> Row, 1986, 1989

PECK, M. Scott
> – *The Road Less Traveled.* Simon & Schuster, 1978
> – *People of the Lie.* Simon & Schuster, 1983

PINK, Daniel
> *A Whole New Mind.* River Head Books
> (Penguin), 2005, 2006

TOLLE, Eckhart
> – *The Power of NOW, A Guide to Spiritual Enlightenment.*
> Namaste Publishing, 1999
> – *Stillness Speaks.* Namaste Publishing, 2003
> – *A New Earth.* Namaste Publishing, 2005

VAN ZANT, Iyanla

 – *In The Meantime.* Simon & Schuster, 1998

 – *Yesterday I Cried.* Simon & Schuster, 1998

 – *Until Today: Daily Devotions for Spiritual Growth & Peace of Mind.* Simon & Schuster, 2000

 – *Every Day I Pray: Prayers for Awakening to the Grace of Inner Communion.* Simon & Schuster, 2001

WALSCH, Neale Donald

 The New Revelations. Atria Books, 2002

WEEMS, Renita

 – *Just a Sister Away.* Lura Media, 1988

 – *Listening For God.* Simon & Shuster, 1999

WILLIAMSON, Marianne.

 A Return to Love. Harper Collins, 1992

ZUKAV, Gary.

 – *Seat of the Soul.* Simon & Schuster, 1989

 – *Heart of the Soul.* Simon & Shuster, 2002

ACKNOWLEDGEMENTS

I am deeply grateful to my husband Ed who has been my greatest mentor, teacher, and partner on my life journey. He has encouraged and steered me onto paths that I would otherwise never have traveled.

I am grateful to my biological family; my parents, Homer and Thelma Payne (deceased), because they were incredible life teachers; my brothers, John, Alan, and Homer David, who helped to provide the context for my early life. We all played our intended roles, and I learned a great deal about who I am through experiences in this family. To other members of my family, I am grateful for your support, Brad, Askari, Heidi, Eric, Ben, Andrew, and Bruce. To stepdaughters from my first marriage, Cynthia, Chandra, and Carla, I am grateful for the many ways that you enriched my life.

I am grateful to Dottie, Bronwen, Delstene, Harvey, Julie, Phyllis, Janet, Elaine, Adele, Sandy, Tom, Brad and Ed for reading and critiquing this manuscript. I am grateful to Elaine for her gifts in graphic design, and Ed for his gift of photography. To Carla Reidel, my editor, I give thanks because you have dared to walk with me on the journey to bring this book to fruition. I thank you all.

This book would not be possible without all of my coaching clients over the last thirty-plus years. Thank you for your willingness to share some of the deepest, most sacred parts of your lives with me. I am humbled and have such gratitude to each of you. It is because of you that I have been able to summon up the strength and courage to write this book. It was truly my honor to be your coach during some of the most challenging times in your lives. Thank you.

But, mostly, I am grateful to God and all of my angels for the gift of life.

ABOUT THE AUTHOR

Sarah Payne Naylor is a life and career coach. Her work includes leadership development and executive coaching as an independent contractor for the Federal Government. She also brings experience in the business environment and non-profit sectors as well as state and national public policy advocacy. Sarah has been a partner in The Naylor Group since it was founded in 1995. Prior to this work she was an assistant director for public policy in the Lutheran Office of Governmental Affairs in Washington, D.C. As a member of the Board of Directors for Lutheran Immigration and Refugee Service, Sarah traveled to refugee camps around the world and has traveled extensively throughout the world for pleasure.

When Sarah is not working as a coach, she works with small groups to facilitate spiritual and personal self-exploration. She also enjoys interior re-design. Other fun pursuits are watercolor painting, sewing, and other needlecrafts such as crocheting and knitting. During her quiet time she enjoys reading spiritual books.

Sarah lives in northern Arizona, near Sedona, with her husband, Ed, and their dog, Sam.

You may contact Sarah at www.crossingroughwaters.com